FEIFFER

THE COLLECTED WORKS

FANTAGRAPHICS BOOKS

Feiffer

THE COLLECTED WORKS

Clifford

FANTAGRAPHICS BOOKS
7563 Lake City Way
Seattle, WA 98115

Editorial coordination: Robert Fiore.
Design and art direction: Dale Crain.
Production assistance: Mark Thompson,
Typesetting: Linda M. Gorell.
Gary Groth and Kim Thompson, Publishers.

Special thanks to Will Eisner, Denis Kitchen, John Benson,
and Peter Kuper for archival material and assistance.

First Fantagraphics Books edition: April, 1988.
1 3 5 7 9 10 8 6 4 2

ISBN (soft): 0-930193-40-7
ISBN (hard): 0-930193-41-5

Printed in Singapore through Palace Press.

Write for a catalogue of Fantgraphics Books releases containing
work by Winsor McCay, E.C. Segar, R. Crumb, Vaughn Bode,
Los Bros. Hernandez, and more cartoon greats past and present.

FOREWORD

Some artists are sprinters and others are long distance runners. The sprinters arrive among us with brilliant displays of skill; they are prodigies, wunderkinder, naturals. For their moment, they appear to leave everyone else behind them and the audience marvels at their originality, their daring, their obvious dominance over the field. Newspapers and magazines chronicle their doings; a seat is opened on the Carson show; the critics make ready a place in Valhalla.

And then they are gone. Their departures are usually as abrupt as their arrivals. And after they're gone, people sometimes speak sadly about what happened, how the wunderkind simply burned out or did not grow or Couldn't Handle It. Sometimes there are bitter laments about the malignant force of the Bitch Goddess Success. More often there is an unhappy understanding that the prodigy only had one or two moves in him and no closing kick at all. But nobody is ever certain; failure is as much a mystery as success. All we know is that they are gone. The sprinters.

Jules Feiffer is a long distance runner. For more than 30 years he has been operating at the highest level of his craft, producing a body of work that ranks with the finest ever produced in this country. His widely syndicated weekly cartoon in the *Village Voice* continues to astonish with its freshness and wit, its ironical insights into urban Americans, its capacity for savage angers. Unlike so many liberals formed in the '40s and '50s, Feiffer hasn't turned his back on his youth or denied his origins; if anything his commitment to social justice is now even deeper than it was when he was young, his loathing of hypocrisy almost Swiftian. Mercifully, he did not become that figure of cliche, the Wised-Up Liberal, panting for a place with the neoconservatives at the Reaganite table. Feiffer is not a neo-anything. Feiffer remains Feiffer.

He is, of course, a fine cartoonist, with a graphic style that seems as natural as handwriting. Like Fred Astaire and Matisse, he creates the illusion that what he does is easy. But his work also proves the contention that the very best cartoonists are always excellent writers. Drawing skill and graphic style are never enough. Consider only the works of such superior writers as George Herriman, Tad Dorgan, Chester Gould, Garry Trudeau, Harold Gray, Hugo Pratt, Billy DeBeck (and such a list could fill several paragraphs) and you realize how much pure language, or a gift for narrative, or the ability to create memorable characters can mean to a cartoonist. In the end, writing was what made Milton Caniff a much greater cartoonist than Noel Sickles; it made the Roy Crane of *Captain Easy*

superior to the Roy Crane of *Buz Sawyer*. So we can admire the way Feiffer lays out a sequence; we can appreciate his gift for build and surprise; we can cherish the way he socks in his blacks and his absolute trust of white space. But we can't ever separate his graphics from his words. If we do, we lose the essential Jules Feiffer.

Those words and pictures, welded together in a single expression, come from a man with a moral intelligence and common sense. He is not an ideologue; he issues no dogmatic strictures about the meaning of life. In his political cartoons, he has only one basic message: he would like the government of the United States to behave better. Husbands, wives, lovers, friends can all behave badly—displaying elastic consciences, self-absorption, personal ruthlessness, a reliance on psycho-babble—and Feiffer can cherish them. We have followed a few of those private Feiffer creations—Bernard Mergendeiler and The Dancer—across the decades. But such people do not command the hydrogen bomb, the armed forces, and the various forms of the secret police. They are powerless and Feiffer has reserved his fiercest onslaughts for those with power. "I can't draw a president I like," he wrote once. "As a political satirist, my pen only works where it can hurt." And like any moral critic worthy of the name, he only hurts those who can hurt him back.

As his work has shown from the beginning, he is most moved to anger by lies, hypocrisy, and sham, and he knows that such sins are not the sole property of the Right. In the '60s, he certainly cut through the flabby self-righteousness of those who claimed to stand on the Left. From Eisenhower to Reagan, no politician was spared, but he was always aware that stupidity and intellectual carelessness were as dangerous when guiding the Weathermen as when they were allied to power in the hands of Johnson or Nixon.

When Feiffer's country does behave, he feels no duty to applaud; his function is not that of a cheerleader. But his sensibility is not narrowly political either. From the first cartoons in the *Voice* in 1956, his eye and ear have engaged the lies, hypocrisy, and sham that are so often at the heart of personal relationships (the last phrase is itself one that Feiffer has speared with his pen). Those social and personal cartoons are considerably less savage and also less dated than the overtly political ones. They show that Feiffer had used his own psychoanalysis to understand others, as well as himself. But his compassion is never maudlin or sentimental; it always has bite, an edge, the distance of the ironist. As he plays the variations on his theme, he sometimes reminds me of a bop musician. He is, of course, always hip. It was no accident that a man with his range (and his understanding of human folly) would begin to strain against the limitations of the weekly cartoon. Soon he was exploring other forms and his artistic restlessness has given us the graphic novel *Tantrum*; his novels *Harry the Rat With Women* and *Ackroyd*; the plays *Little Murders*, *The White House Murder Case*, *Knock, Knock,* and *Grown-Ups*; screenplays for the movies *Carnal Knowledge* and *Popeye*.

These were not mere extensions of the weekly cartoon; but they were *always* products of the complex talent that made those cartoons so superior. He wrote them out of the same personal sensibility, the same view of the world; not one of them could be dismissed as a job. My own feeling is that the novels, plays, and movies have helped make the cartoons even more brilliant. In the weekly cartoons, Feiffer always works within the limitations of the form; he doesn't try to make them what they can never be. He seemed to know from the start that if the cartoonist wants to extend his range, he must move on and write a novel, a play, a movie. His example proves that this can be done without abandoning cartooning; if anything, the disciplines nourish each other. The mystery is that so few cartoonists have done what Feiffer has done. Surely, Caniff, Crane, Will Eisner, among others, could have been wonderful movie directors. But it takes a special kind of crazy courage for a man acclaimed in one discipline to risk falling on his ass in another. Feiffer is a brave man.

The extraordinary thing about Feiffer now is that there are no signs of an erosion of energy, no compromises in the integrity of the work. The history of cartooning is full of examples of men who started out with brilliance and passion, and then slowly handed over their work to assistants, while they took the bows for work that was no longer theirs. That will never happen to Feiffer. His work is made by hand; it doesn't come off the rack. As we move toward the end of this dreadful century, one of the consolations of the passage will surely be the continued presence of Feiffer. The long distance runner will be there in our lives, gazing at our pretensions and our flaws, savaging those whose cruelty and stupidity poison the country and the world, and all the while making us laugh with the fearful shock of recognition. This series will acknowledge the breadth and power of Feiffer's achievement; it will provide a detailed record of the career and the times; and it will be one of the answers given when the children of the next century ask why so many men and women in ours remained silent in the face of enormous lies. Feiffer proves that not all of us were quiet. All did not take the king's shilling. Some ran the whole race, and Feiffer was one of them.

—PETE HAMILL

PREFACE

From childhood on Jules Feiffer never had the slightest doubt what his career would be. Where other comic strip readers idolized the characters, to Feiffer the real supermen were the cartoonists:

> *"To me these men were heroes. The world they lived in, as I saw it in those years of idolatry, was a world in which a person was blessedly in control of his own existence: wrote what he wanted to write, drew it the way he wanted to draw it—and was, by definition, brilliant. And thus, loved by millions. It was a logical extension of my own world—except the results were a lot better. Instead of being little and consequently ridiculed for staying in the house all day and drawing pictures, one was big, and consequently canonized for staying in the house all day and drawing pictures. Instead of having no friends because one stayed in the house all day and drew pictures, one grew up and had millions of friends because one stayed in the house all day and drew pictures. Instead of being small and skinny with no muscles and no power because one stayed in the house all day and drew pictures, one grew up to be less small, less skinny, still perhaps with no muscles, but with lots of power: a friend of Presidents and board chairmen; an intimate of movie stars and ball players—all because one stayed in the house all day and drew pictures."*

(From *The Great Comic Book Heroes*)

In 1946 the 17-year-old Feiffer made his first concrete step toward joining those heroic ranks when he landed a job with Will Eisner as an assistant on *The Spirit Section*, an eight-page "comic book insert" syndicated to newspapers. More than an employer, Eisner was one of Feiffer's greatest boyhood idols. This unusual employer/employee relationship would serve both men well in coming years. Feiffer started out doing the dirty work: ruling panel borders, filling in blacks, signing Eisner's signature ("I was immediately better at it than he was," thanks to years of imitation). Eisner's staff would contract whenever the number of subscribing papers went down, but Feiffer managed to hold on. "The main reason he kept me on was because I was the only real fan he had. I mean, the others in the office in the early days, [Jerry] Grandinetti, [John] Spranger, would talk about how old-fashioned he was, and would put down the work as terribly dated. I didn't know what the hell they were talking about. I

thought this was the most wonderful stuff I had ever seen in my life. And whatever other annoying and wise-guy features I had which pissed Eisner off, he also knew I was a scholar of his work, that I was a groupie. That certainly didn't hurt his feelings. To the others, this was a job, and if they left it, they'd go on to another job; this was an obsession with me." Years later Feiffer would return the favor, bringing Eisner back into the public eye with his book *The Great Comic Book Heroes*, which led to a general revival of Eisner's work.

The main feature of the section was *The Spirit*, a hard-boiled detective strip with Runyonesque overtones. As time went on Feiffer became more and more involved in the writing of the strip. "At some point," Feiffer says, "we got into one of our arguments—and we got into a lot of them—about his stories. I said that his post-'46 stories weren't really up to his '39, '40, and '41 stories [Eisner left the series to join the army during World War II]. He had heard enough of this, and he said, if you think you can do better, write me a story. So I did. He liked it, and from that point on I was writing a lot of them." Feiffer feels that he had so internalized Eisner's style of writing that "even when Eisner had nothing to do with it, [it was] still essentially his...I was simply acting as Eisner's head, doing them as I knew Eisner would do them, or would have done them at an earlier time."

Feiffer got to use his own head in the summer of 1949. "I was making $25 a week...I was writing *The Spirit* and laying it out. I thought that was worth $30 a week. [Eisner] informed me that it really wasn't, so I threatened to quit." To keep him on, Eisner offered the back page of the section to do his own strip, which turned out to be *Clifford*.

Clifford had been the title character in Feiffer's first published strip, a two-pager in an abortive Eisner comic book project called *Kewpies*. The original story left Clifford floating away on a gum bubble. The new version brought him back to earth, less gangly, more rounded, and apparently a bit younger. Although it was calculated to be commercially acceptable, there was a distinctly personal element to it. "I wanted to do a kid strip that was unabashedly pro-kid and from a kid's point of view. It seemed to me that every strip done on kids up to that time was done from an adult point of view, saying, 'Aren't they terrible, aren't they awful.'" Unlike most kid strip characters, Clifford's is very much a city childhood, and specifically a New York City childhood, one of shabby genteel apartments, corner candy stores, vacant lot playgrounds, and shouted conversations from the street to the third floor. (Once when Eisner was feeling a deadline pinch, Clifford even took over *The Spirit*, with a parody of the previous year's stories.)

The childhood theme must have been in the air at the time; 1950 saw the debut of Charles Schulz's *Peanuts* and 1951 the debut of Hank Ketcham's *Dennis the Menace*. At the same time Feiffer began work on a proposal for a daily strip called *Kermit*. At age 22, the course of Feiffer's life could easily have been set. Though he hadn't yet figured out a way into the big time, he had the makings of a slick, salable style, commercial subject matter, and three years experience turning out a weekly gag strip. But in 1951 his course was changed drastically, courtesy of the draft board. By the time the army was through with Feiffer and Feiffer was through with the army, he was no longer willing to keep his personal convictions in the background of his work. When he returned to civilian life the *Spirit Section* was long gone, and Feiffer had a very different kid strip in the works—*Munro*.   —*ROBERT FIORE*

[Quotes are taken from *The Great Comic Book Heroes*, an interview conducted by John Benson for *Panels* magazine, and an interview conducted by Gary Groth for *The Comics Journal*.]

Clifford

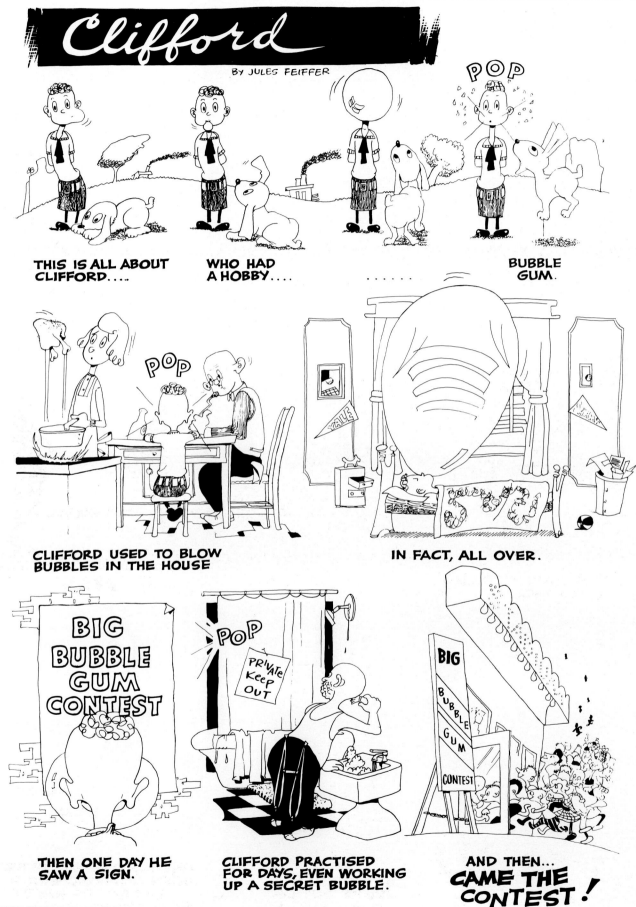

Clifford

BY JULES FEIFFER

THIS IS ALL ABOUT CLIFFORD.....

WHO HAD A HOBBY....

....

BUBBLE GUM.

CLIFFORD USED TO BLOW BUBBLES IN THE HOUSE

IN FACT, ALL OVER.

THEN ONE DAY HE SAW A SIGN.

CLIFFORD PRACTISED FOR DAYS, EVEN WORKING UP A SECRET BUBBLE.

AND THEN... CAME THE CONTEST!

FEIFFER'S FIRST PUBLISHED STRIP, FROM *KEWPIES* (SPRING 1949).

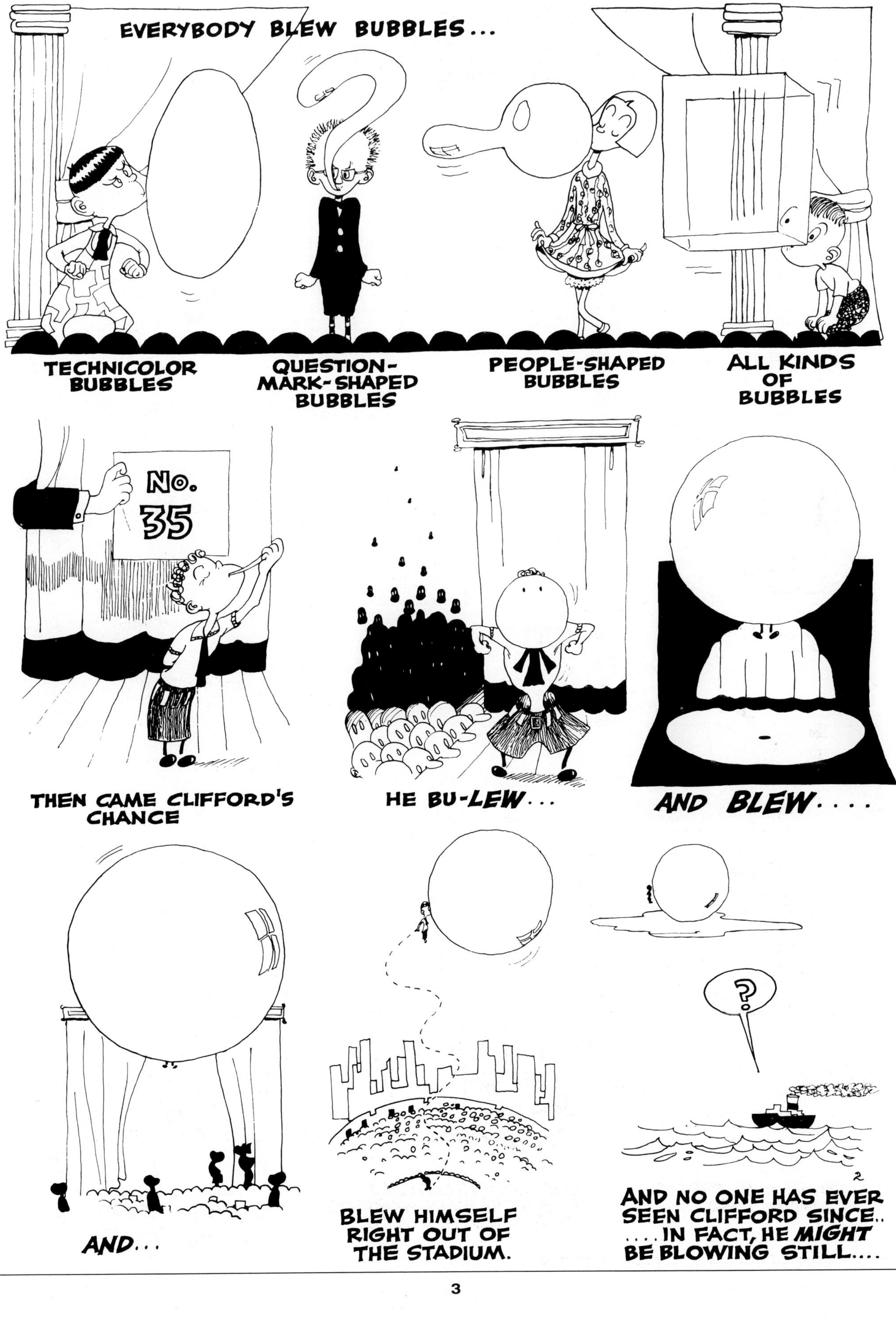
EVERYBODY BLEW BUBBLES...
TECHNICOLOR BUBBLES
QUESTION-MARK-SHAPED BUBBLES
PEOPLE-SHAPED BUBBLES
ALL KINDS OF BUBBLES
No. 35
THEN CAME CLIFFORD'S CHANCE
HE BU-LEW...
AND BLEW....
AND...
BLEW HIMSELF RIGHT OUT OF THE STADIUM.
?
AND NO ONE HAS EVER SEEN CLIFFORD SINCE..
....IN FACT, HE MIGHT BE BLOWING STILL....

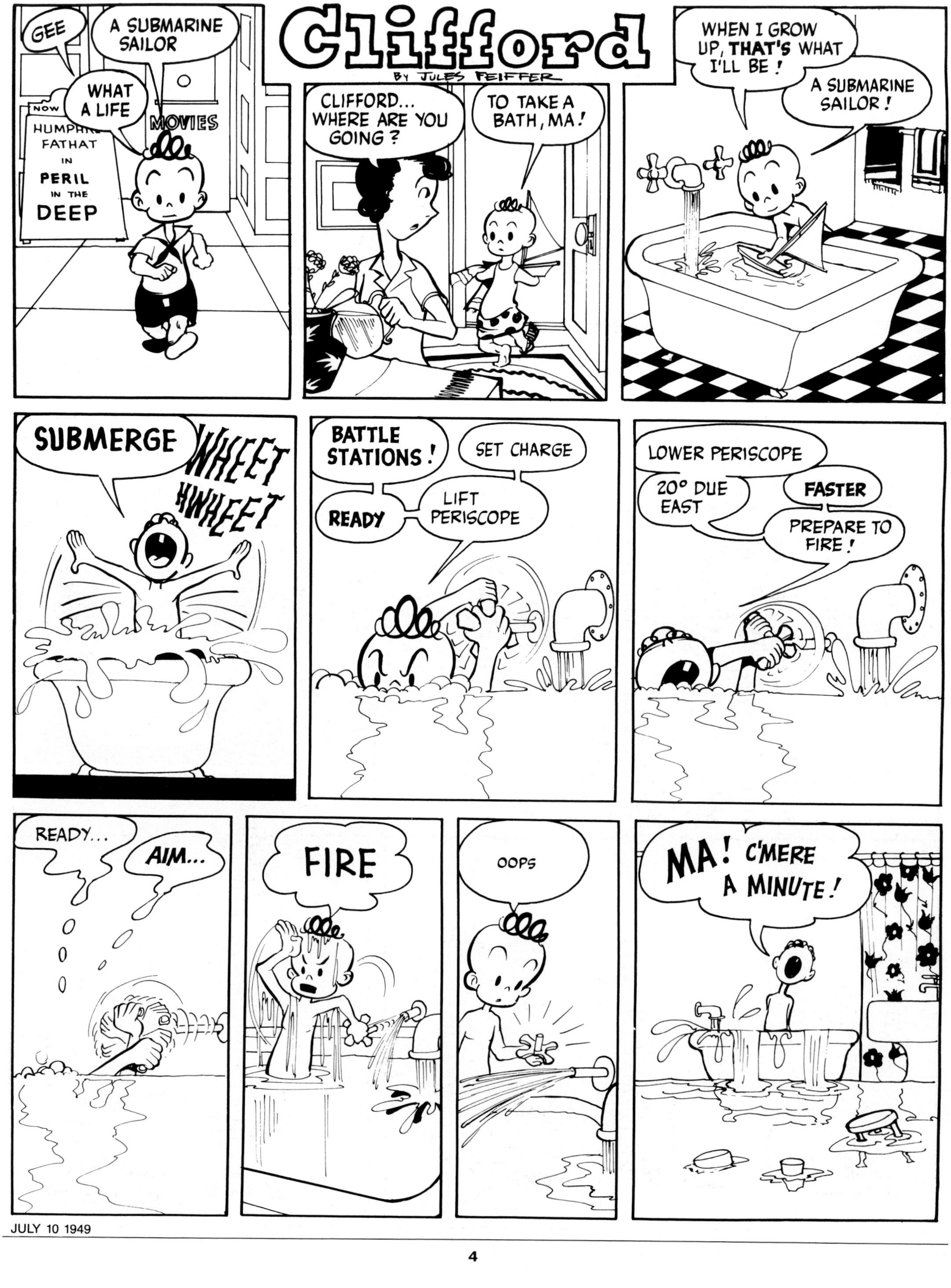
Clifford
BY JULES FEIFFER
GEE
A SUBMARINE SAILOR
WHAT A LIFE
NOW
HUMPHR
FATHAT
IN
PERIL
IN THE
DEEP
MOVIES
CLIFFORD... WHERE ARE YOU GOING?
TO TAKE A BATH, MA!
WHEN I GROW UP, THAT'S WHAT I'LL BE!
A SUBMARINE SAILOR!
SUBMERGE
WHEET HWHEET
BATTLE STATIONS!
SET CHARGE
READY
LIFT PERISCOPE
LOWER PERISCOPE
20° DUE EAST
FASTER
PREPARE TO FIRE!
READY...
AIM...
FIRE
OOPS
MA! C'MERE A MINUTE!

JULY 10 1949

Clifford

BY JULES FEIFFER

JULY 17 1949

Clifford
BY JULES FEIFFER

NOW REMEMBER, CLIFFORD, YOU'RE SICK! STAY IN BED! READ A BOOK!

CAPTAIN GORE

"...WITH THE GRACEFUL EASE OF A JUNGLE CAT, CAPTAIN CLIFFORD CRAWLED THROUGH THE JUNGLE..."

"..SOFTLY, WITH THE GRACEFUL EASE OF A JUNGLE CAT, CAPTAIN CLIFFORD LIFTED HIS HEAD ABOVE THE BUSHES AND PEERED AT THE VAST SEA BELOW."

"CAUTIOUSLY, CAPTAIN CLIFFORD PERCHED HIMSELF ON THE EDGE OF THE CLIFF..."

THUD

"AS THE SUN SLOWLY SANK BENEATH THE TREES, CAPTAIN CLIFFORD, WITH THE GRACEFUL EASE OF A JUNGLE CAT, RETIRED TO HIS TENT TO THINK THINGS OVER."

CAPTAIN GORE

JULY 24 1949

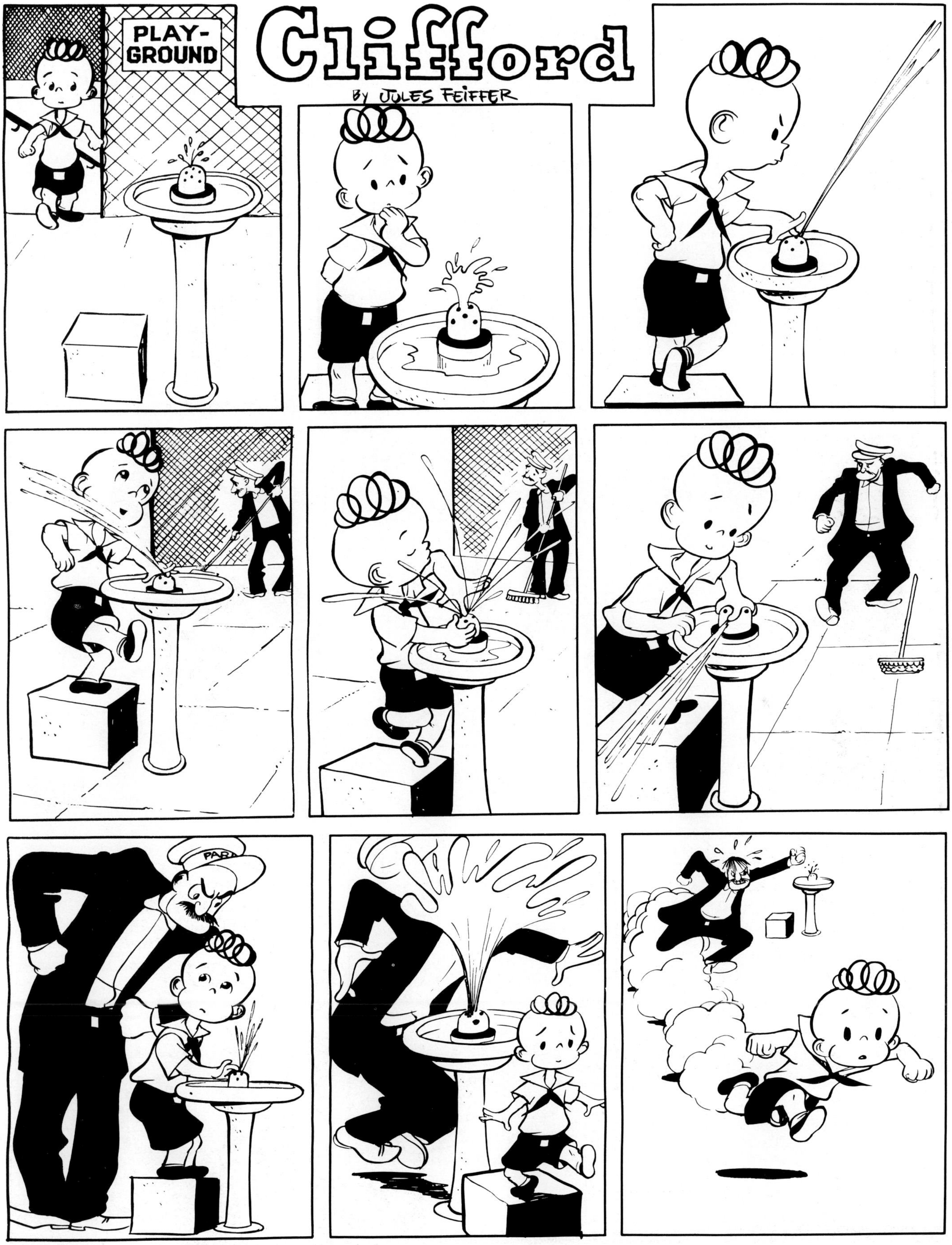
PLAY-
GROUND
Clifford
BY JULES FEIFFER

JULY 31 1949

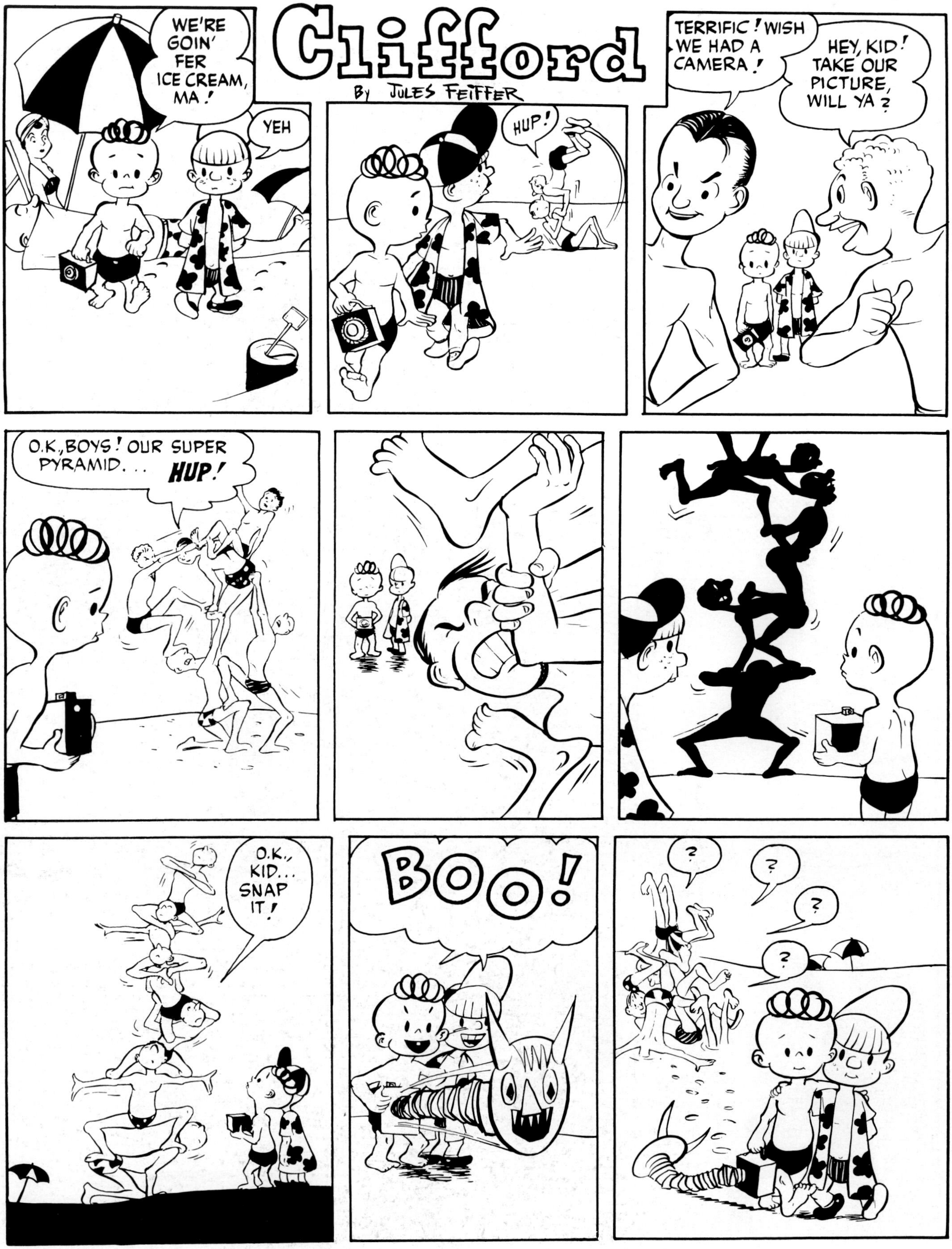
Clifford
By Jules Feiffer
WE'RE GOIN' FER ICE CREAM, MA!
YEH
HUP!
TERRIFIC! WISH WE HAD A CAMERA!
HEY, KID! TAKE OUR PICTURE, WILL YA?
O.K., BOYS! OUR SUPER PYRAMID... HUP!
O.K., KID... SNAP IT!
BOO!
?
?
?
?

AUGUST 7 1949

Clifford

BY JULES FEIFFER

WHAT A GAME, FOLKS... WINSLOW ON FIRST, FRY ON SECOND, TWO OUT, AND THREE-AND-ONE THE COUNT ON THE BATTER, JOE SHEA.

THERE'S THE PITCH... STRIKE TWO... A FAST BALL RIGHT OVER!

IT'S THE LAST HALF OF THE NINTH... OUR SIDE BEHIND BY ONE RUN... THE WINNING RUN ON FIRST....

THE PAYOFF PITCH COMING UP... JAXON READY... INTO HIS MOTION... WAIT!.. SHEA STEPS OUT OF THE BOX...

THIS IS A TENSE WAR OF NERVES GOING ON BEFORE THESE 60,000 SCREAMING FANS... ALL RIGHT NOW... SHEA BACK IN...

A WALK WILL BRING UP SLUGGER GINCH... A SINGLE WILL TIE IT ALL UP... JAXON INTO THE WINDUP...

RUNNERS LEAD OFF... FRY AT SECOND, WINSLOW AT FIRST... WITH TWO OUT, THEY'LL RUN ON ANYTHING... SHEA IN HIS QUESTION-MARK STANCE..THERE GO THE RUNNERS...

THERE'S THE PITCH!!

CLICK

WHAT'S WRONG WITH CLIFFORD? HE'S JUST BEEN STANDING THAT WAY FOR THE LAST TEN MINUTES!

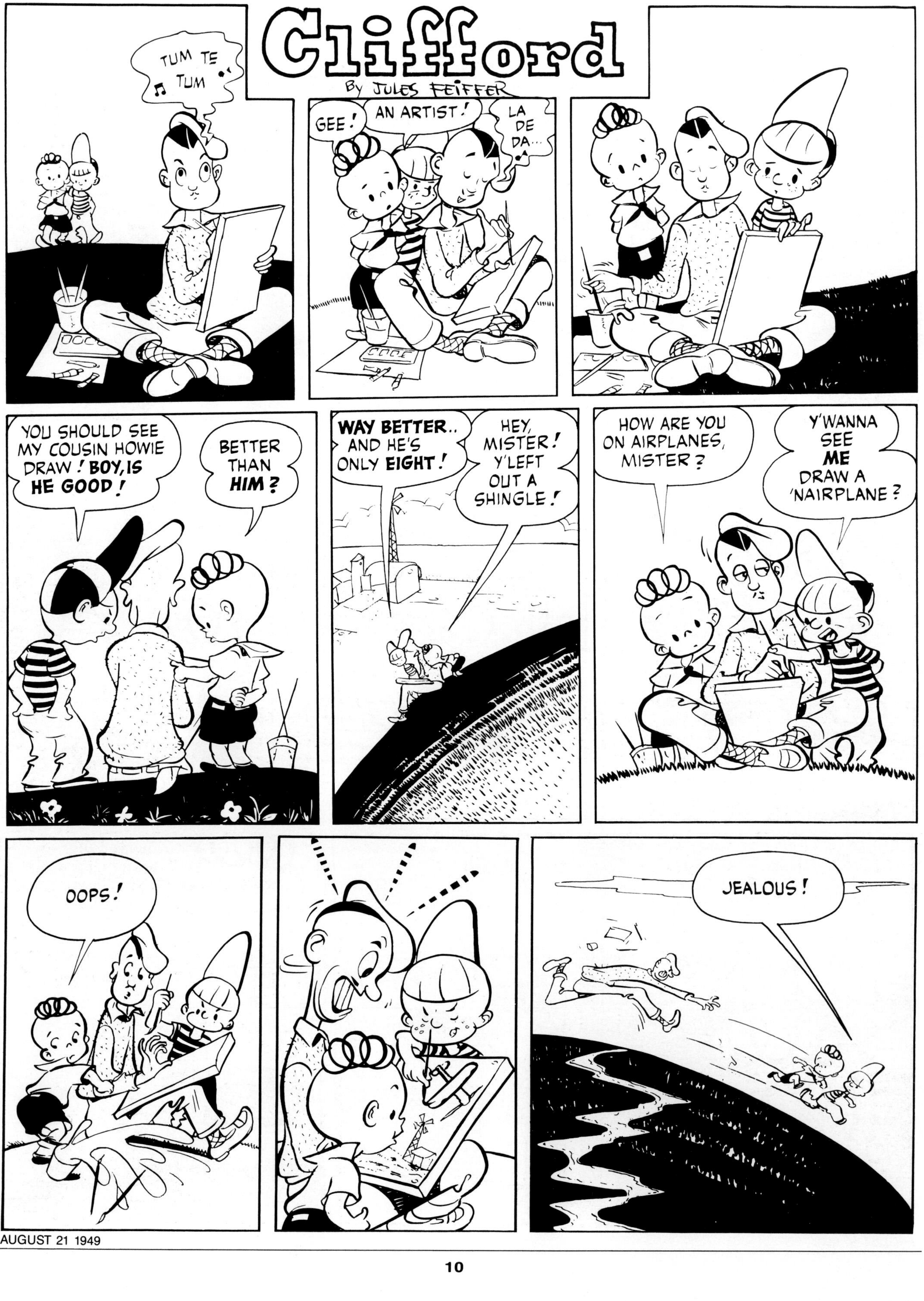
Clifford
By Jules Feiffer
TUM TE TUM
GEE!
AN ARTIST!
LA DE DA...
YOU SHOULD SEE MY COUSIN HOWIE DRAW! BOY, IS HE GOOD!
BETTER THAN HIM?
WAY BETTER.. AND HE'S ONLY EIGHT!
HEY, MISTER! Y'LEFT OUT A SHINGLE!
HOW ARE YOU ON AIRPLANES, MISTER?
Y'WANNA SEE ME DRAW A 'NAIRPLANE?
OOPS!
JEALOUS!

AUGUST 21 1949

Clifford

BY JULES FEIFFER

AUGUST 28 1949

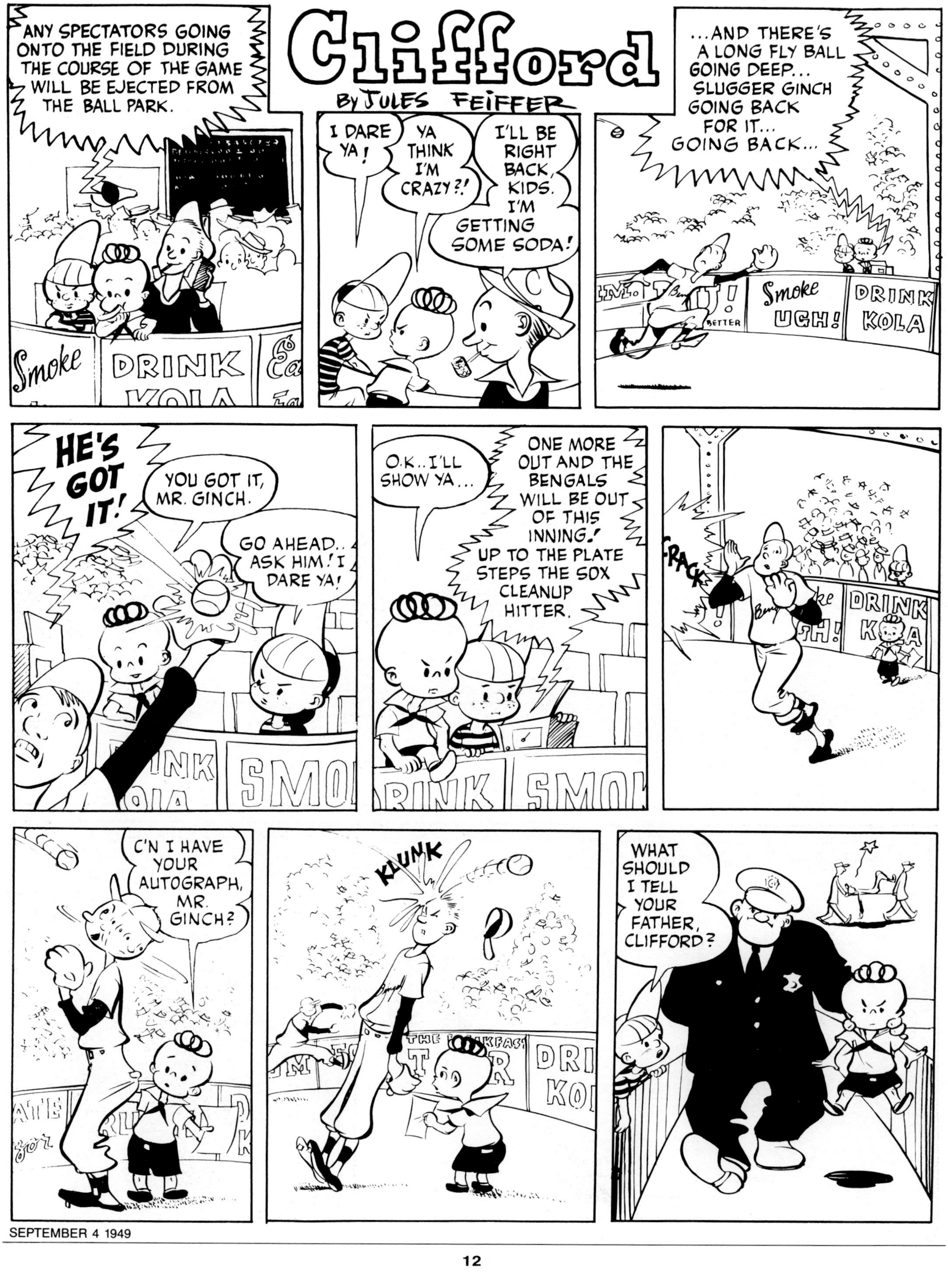
Clifford
By Jules Feiffer
ANY SPECTATORS GOING ONTO THE FIELD DURING THE COURSE OF THE GAME WILL BE EJECTED FROM THE BALL PARK.
I DARE YA!
YA THINK I'M CRAZY?!
I'LL BE RIGHT BACK, KIDS. I'M GETTING SOME SODA!
...AND THERE'S A LONG FLY BALL GOING DEEP... SLUGGER GINCH GOING BACK FOR IT... GOING BACK...
HE'S GOT IT!
YOU GOT IT, MR. GINCH.
GO AHEAD.. ASK HIM! I DARE YA!
O.K.. I'LL SHOW YA...
ONE MORE OUT AND THE BENGALS WILL BE OUT OF THIS INNING! UP TO THE PLATE STEPS THE SOX CLEANUP HITTER.
CRACK
C'N I HAVE YOUR AUTOGRAPH, MR. GINCH?
KLUNK
WHAT SHOULD I TELL YOUR FATHER, CLIFFORD?

SEPTEMBER 4 1949

Clifford
BY JULES FEIFFER

SEPTEMBER 11 1949

13

Clifford
By JULES FEIFFER

BOY, HAVE I GOT NERVE!

BET I GOT MORE NERVE 'N ANY KID!

HI YA, CLIFFORD!

WANNA SEE ME SWALLOW A LIVE GRASSHOPPER?

GO 'WAY, SEYMOUR. I'M DOIN' MY HOMEWORK!

WATCH!!! I'M DRINKIN' FILTHY WATER!

$$\begin{array}{r} 10 \\ +6 \\ \hline 16 \\ -8 \\ \hline 8 \end{array}$$

I C'N BEAT UP ANY GIRL ONNA BLOCK!

WANT T'SEE ME TURN OVER A BABY CARRIAGE?

NO PARKING

I C'N...

$$\begin{array}{r} 16 \\ \times 2 \\ \hline 36 \\ 34 \\ 32 \end{array}$$

WHACK

WAHHH

SEYMOUR, YOU'RE A HORRIBLE, MEAN, BAD LITTLE BOY! I'M GOING TO TELL YOUR MOTHER ON YOU!

SIGH... SOMETIMES I GOT SO MUCH NERVE, IT FRIGHTENS ME!

?

SEPTEMBER 18 1949

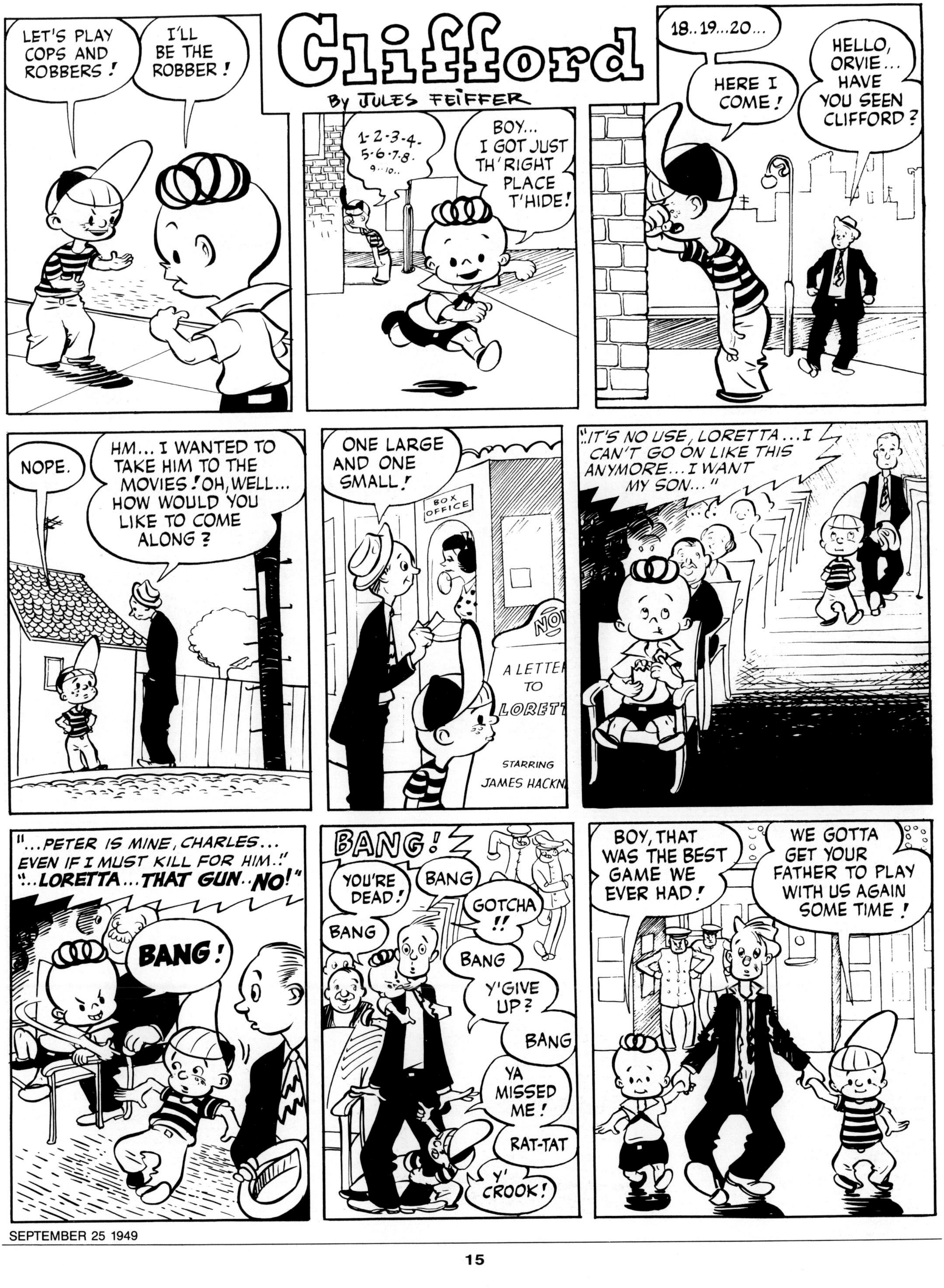
LET'S PLAY COPS AND ROBBERS!
I'LL BE THE ROBBER!
Clifford
BY JULES FEIFFER
1-2-3-4-5-6-7-8-9...10...
BOY... I GOT JUST TH' RIGHT PLACE T'HIDE!
18..19...20...
HERE I COME!
HELLO, ORVIE... HAVE YOU SEEN CLIFFORD?
NOPE.
HM... I WANTED TO TAKE HIM TO THE MOVIES! OH, WELL... HOW WOULD YOU LIKE TO COME ALONG?
ONE LARGE AND ONE SMALL!
BOX OFFICE
A LETTER TO LORETT
STARRING
JAMES HACKN
"...IT'S NO USE, LORETTA...I CAN'T GO ON LIKE THIS ANYMORE...I WANT MY SON..."
"...PETER IS MINE, CHARLES... EVEN IF I MUST KILL FOR HIM..!"
"...LORETTA...THAT GUN..NO!"
BANG!
BANG!
YOU'RE DEAD!
BANG
GOTCHA!!
BANG
BANG
Y'GIVE UP?
BANG
YA MISSED ME!
RAT-TAT
Y' CROOK!
BOY, THAT WAS THE BEST GAME WE EVER HAD!
WE GOTTA GET YOUR FATHER TO PLAY WITH US AGAIN SOME TIME!

SEPTEMBER 25 1949

Clifford
BY JULES FEIFFER

Clifford CRASH

BY JULES FEIFFER

Clifford
BY JULES FEIFFER

OCTOBER 16 1949

Clifford

BY JULES FEIFFER

OCTOBER 23 1949

Clifford
BY JULES FEIFFER

NOW... REMEMBER, CLIFFORD... BE NICE TO COUSIN IRWIN WHEN HE COMES! HE HAS A VERY DEEP INFERIORITY COMPLEX!

WHAT'S THAT?

OOPS... THAT'S HIM NOW!

I BROUGHT MY CAMERA...

COME IN, IRWIN.

YEH.. BUT WHAT'S AN...

IT'S A MICRORANGE SUPER XXXXX VANICO FILTER WITH FLASHBULB ATTACHMENT! YOU WOULDN'T WANT TO POSE... WOULD YOU...?

THAT SOUNDS VERY NICE, IRWIN! HOW IS YOUR MOTHER?

I'VE BEEN TRYING TO GET SOME INTERESTING SHOTS FOR MY SAMPLE CASE WHEN I GO TO TRY OUT AS A MOVIE DIRECTOR. BUT.. I GUESS.. YOU DON'T WANT TO POSE...

WHY, WE'D **LOVE** TO, IRWIN!

THIS WILL BE A COMBINATION ANGLE SHOT AND CHARACTER STUDY SHOWING THE FRUSTRATED DESIRES OF A MIDDLE CLASS FAMILY IN OUR MODERN SOCIETY!

NOBODY MOVE.

I'LL ALLOW AN $^{F}/200$ EXPOSURE WITH A $\frac{1}{8}\frac{\sqrt{20}}{.6}$ LENS RANGE...

ALLOWING FOR..

DING

DOOR BELL.

HIYA GANG!

HMM... I'LL ALLOW AN $^{F}/200$ EXPOSURE WITH A $\frac{1}{8}\frac{\sqrt{20}}{.6}$ LENS...

WOW! I'M MISSING H.V. KETTLEDRUM!!

..AND SO ON THE ONE HAND WE SEE CHINA AND ON THE OTHER WE SEE ARGENTINA AND ON THE OTHER WE SEE...

I'LL ALLOW AN $^{F}/200$ EXPOSURE...

OOOH! MY COOKING!

WHAT'S THAT?

MY COUSIN. HE'S GOT COMPLEXES!

$^{F}/200$ EXPOSURE? ...LENS RANGE? ..FOCAL LENGTH? ANYBODY... WANT TO EAT.. A... CAMERA...?

OCTOBER 30 1949

Clifford
BY JULES FEIFFER

NOVEMBER 6 1949

Clifford
BY JULES FEIFFER

NOVEMBER 13 1949

Clifford
By Jules Feiffer

NOVEMBER 20 1949

Clifford

By Jules Feiffer

SNOW!

HEY ORVIE! SNOW!

YEAH!

MA! WHERE'S MY SLED? WHERE'S MY WINTER COAT?

HEY, HINKY... LOOK!

WOW!

WHERE'S MY GALOSHES, MY SHOVEL, MY... HEY, MA!!

LET'S SEE... UMBRELLA... HIP BOOTS... EYE GLASS PROTECTOR ...EAR STOPS...

IT STOPPED!

HECK! THERE AIN'T EVEN ENOUGH SNOW TO DO ANYTHING WITH!

NOVEMBER 27 1949

Clifford
BY JULES FEIFFER

DECEMBER 4 1949

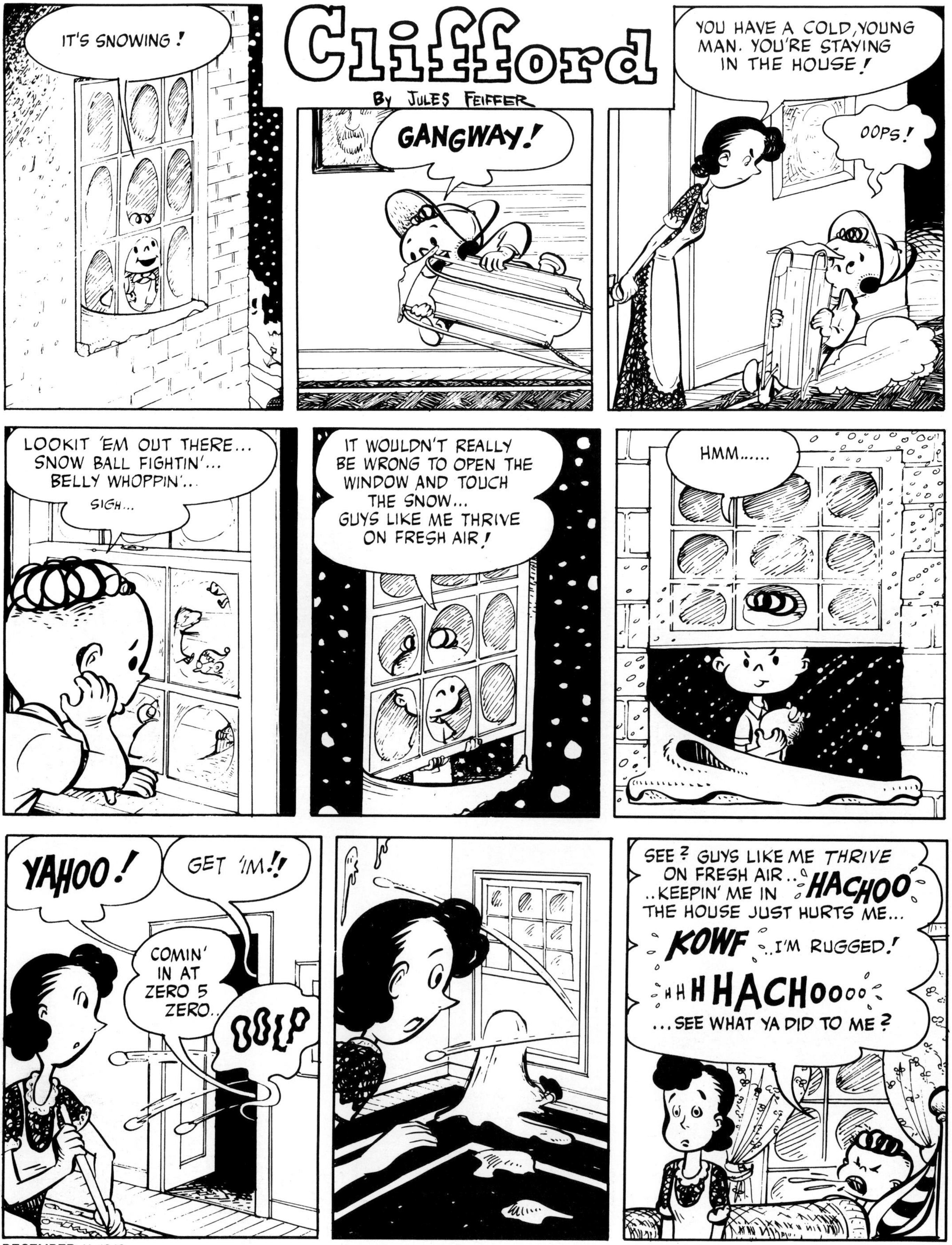
IT'S SNOWING!
Clifford
By Jules Feiffer
GANGWAY!
YOU HAVE A COLD, YOUNG MAN. YOU'RE STAYING IN THE HOUSE!
OOPS!
LOOKIT 'EM OUT THERE... SNOW BALL FIGHTIN'... BELLY WHOPPIN'..
SIGH...
IT WOULDN'T REALLY BE WRONG TO OPEN THE WINDOW AND TOUCH THE SNOW... GUYS LIKE ME THRIVE ON FRESH AIR!
HMM......
YAHOO!
GET 'IM!!
COMIN' IN AT ZERO 5 ZERO..
OOLP
SEE? GUYS LIKE ME THRIVE ON FRESH AIR.. HACHOO ..KEEPIN' ME IN THE HOUSE JUST HURTS ME... KOWF ..I'M RUGGED! HHHHACHOoooo ...SEE WHAT YA DID TO ME?

DECEMBER 11 1949

Clifford
BY JULES FEIFFER

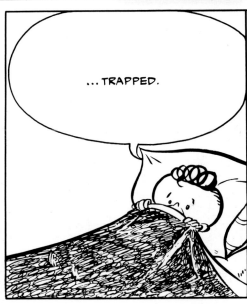

DECEMBER 18 1949

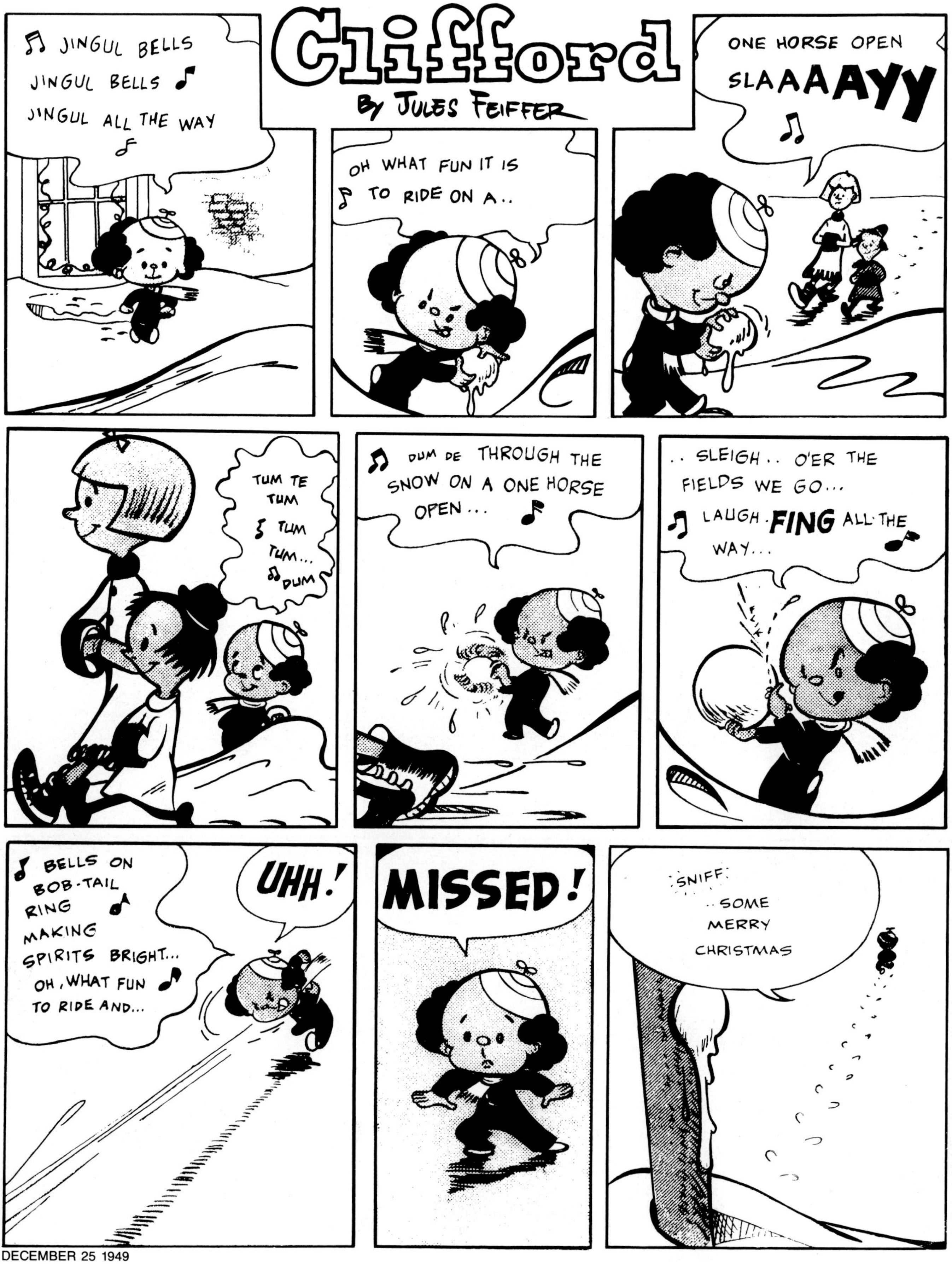
Clifford
By Jules Feiffer
JINGUL BELLS JINGUL BELLS JINGUL ALL THE WAY
OH WHAT FUN IT IS TO RIDE ON A..
ONE HORSE OPEN SLAAAAYY
TUM TE TUM TUM TUM... DUM
DUM DE THROUGH THE SNOW ON A ONE HORSE OPEN...
.. SLEIGH .. O'ER THE FIELDS WE GO... LAUGH·FING ALL·THE WAY...
FLIK
BELLS ON BOB-TAIL RING MAKING SPIRITS BRIGHT... OH, WHAT FUN TO RIDE AND...
UHH!
MISSED!
SNIFF
..SOME MERRY CHRISTMAS

DECEMBER 25 1949

Clifford

By Jules Feiffer

HAPPY NEW YEAR.

SO?

GREAT WEEK!

GREAT!

LOTTA FUN... THAT SNOWBALL FIGHTIN' MONDAY... HINKY GETTIN' HIS FACE WASHED..

YEP.

I STILL SAY WE SHOULDA WON THAT FOOTBALL GAME WEDNESDAY. SEYMOUR ON'Y TOUCHED ME WITH ONE HAND!

. . WE SHOULDA.

AND YESTERDAY... BELLYWHOPPIN' DOWN GLOOVER STREET... WHAT A HILL!

GREAT HILL.

WHAT A WEEK!

GREAT WEEK.

ISN'T IT WONDERFUL, NATALIE? TOMORROW WE HAVE SCHOOL AGAIN!

SIGH...

SIGH...

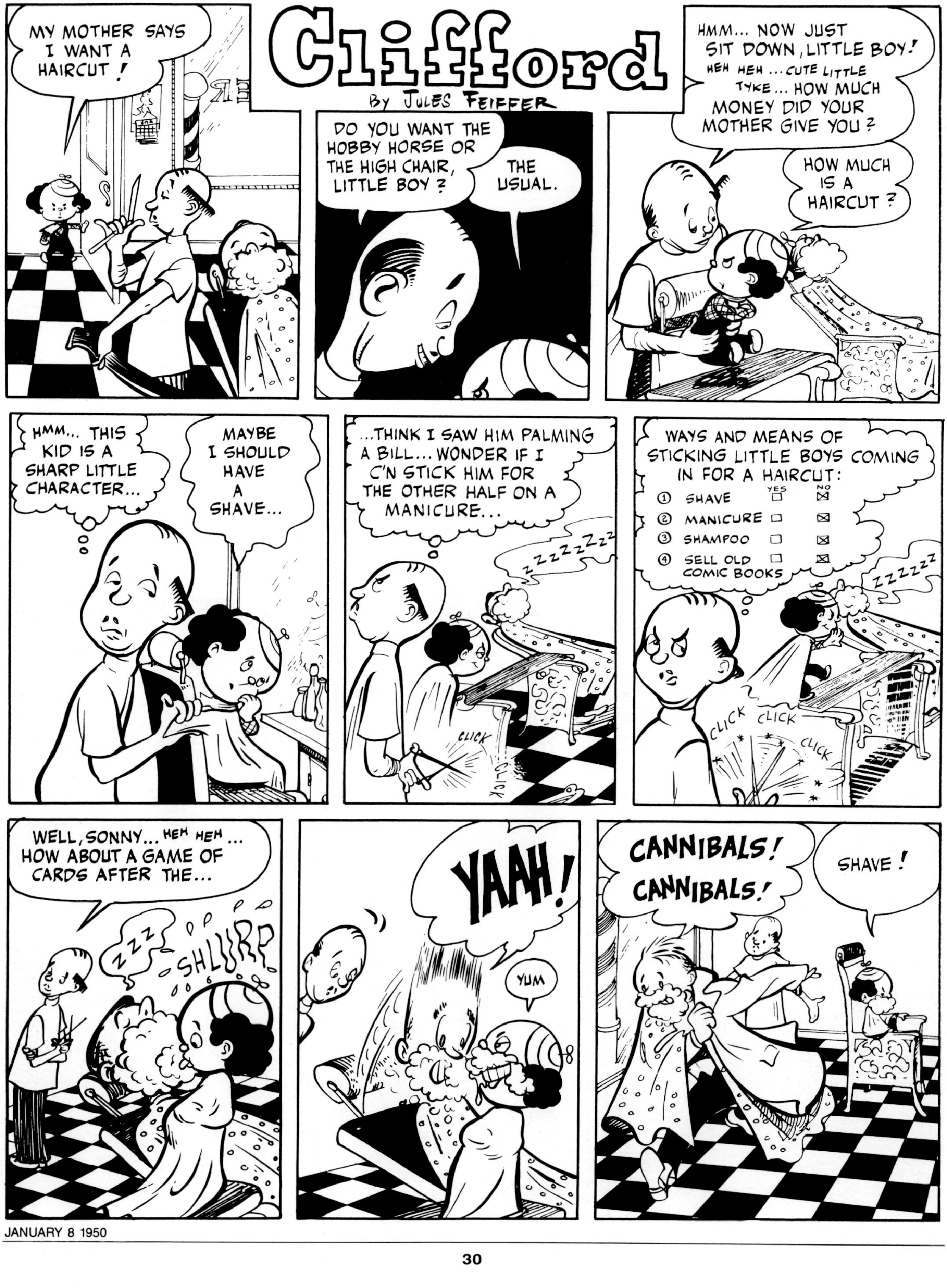
Clifford
By Jules Feiffer
MY MOTHER SAYS I WANT A HAIRCUT!
DO YOU WANT THE HOBBY HORSE OR THE HIGH CHAIR, LITTLE BOY?
THE USUAL.
HMM... NOW JUST SIT DOWN, LITTLE BOY! HEH HEH ...CUTE LITTLE TYKE... HOW MUCH MONEY DID YOUR MOTHER GIVE YOU?
HOW MUCH IS A HAIRCUT?
HMM... THIS KID IS A SHARP LITTLE CHARACTER...
MAYBE I SHOULD HAVE A SHAVE...
...THINK I SAW HIM PALMING A BILL... WONDER IF I C'N STICK HIM FOR THE OTHER HALF ON A MANICURE...
ZZZZZZZZ
CLICK
CLICK
WAYS AND MEANS OF STICKING LITTLE BOYS COMING IN FOR A HAIRCUT:
YES NO
① SHAVE
② MANICURE
③ SHAMPOO
④ SELL OLD COMIC BOOKS
ZZZZZZ
CLICK CLICK CLICK CLICK
WELL, SONNY... HEH HEH ... HOW ABOUT A GAME OF CARDS AFTER THE...
ZZZ
SHLURP
YAAH!
YUM
CANNIBALS! CANNIBALS!
SHAVE!

JANUARY 8 1950

Clifford
BY JULES FEIFFER

T.V. PRESENTS
The TINY TOT
SHOW

HELLO! TINY TOTS, THIS IS YOUR UNCLE BIG TOT SAYING WELCOME TO ANOTHER TINY TOT SESSION.

♪ WELCOME, WELCOME, WELCOME ALL YOU TINY TOTS ♪ WELCOME WELCOME WELCOME YOU DARLING LITTLE WHAT NOTS ♪ WELCOME WELCOME WELC...

CLICK

THE BAR Q BELONG T'ME, CODY!

YEAH?

YEAH!

YEAH?

YEAH!

CLICK

HERE IN THE BALMY TROPIC PARADISE, MOTHER NATURE HAS PLANTED THE MANGANESE OXIDE SWILCHICLEAN PLANT WHICH IN ITS CULTIVATED STATE PROVIDES US WITH...

CLICK

FOLD TWO EGGS AND MIX...THEN ADD FOUR HEAPING TABLESPOONS OF "MOTHER WHIPPETY'S" HOME-MADE BUTTERSCOTCH PIE... BASTE AND...

CLICK

I'M GOIN' IN T'DO MY HOMEWORK, MA!

JANUARY 15 1950

Clifford

BY JULES FEIFFER

JANUARY 22 1950

Clifford
BY JULES FEIFFER

JANUARY 29 1950

WELCOME TO ANOTHER BROADCAST FROM THE MUNICIPAL OPERA. TODAY'S PRESENTATION IS STROMBOLI'S "LA BOPEEP". NOW, BEFORE THE CURTAIN RISES, HERE IS A BRIEF SUMMARY OF ACT I.

VALDICCI, A STARVING POET, LIVES IN A FISHING VILLAGE ENJOYING THE CONTENTED LIFE OF A PEASANT UNTIL HIS FATHER, STEFONI, IS MURDERED BY THE WICKED DUKE...

IT IS THEN THAT MARGUERITTE FLEES TO THE MONASTERY AND IS BRUTALLY SLAIN... WHEREUPON RODOLPHO SWEARS HIS VENGEANCE!

AT THIS MOMENT RHADAMES KILLS RIGONNO AFTER THE CRUEL STRANGLING OF LUCIA. THEN, AS VALDICCI HOLDS THE LIFELESS BODY OF HIS BELOVED MIMI IN HIS ARMS, AND CRIES FOR MERCY FROM THE HANGMAN, THE FIRST ACT CURTAIN FALLS.

CLICK

I BETCHA HE SHOOTS THE HANGMAN AN' ESCAPES!

NAH, THEY'RE GONNA KILL HIM!

BOY.. I C'N HARDLY WAIT FOR THE NEXT ACT!

FEBRUARY 5 1950

Clifford

By JULES FEIFFER

CLIFFORD, YOU'VE BEEN A BAD BOY... I WANT YOU TO SIT THERE WITH YOUR HANDS CLASPED AND **DON'T MOVE!**

...I THINK I'VE GOT AN ITCH...

...IT'S MY NOSE...

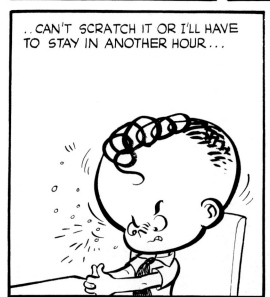

..CAN'T SCRATCH IT OR I'LL HAVE TO STAY IN ANOTHER HOUR...

NOW IT'S MY SHOULDER...

I MUST BE ALLERGIC...IT'S ON MY **TOE** NOW...

ALL RIGHT, CLIFFORD! YOU'VE STAYED LONG ENOUGH...YOU CAN GO HOME NOW!

AAAH

SCRATCH SCRATCH SCRATCH SCRATCH *SCRATCH*

Clifford

BY JULES FEIFFER

FEBRUARY 19 1950

Clifford
BY JULES FEIFFER

FEBRUARY 26 1950

Clifford

BY JULES FEIFFER

CLIFFORD, WILL YOU TAKE THE BOARD ERASERS INTO THE COURT YARD AND CLEAN THEM, PLEASE?

GRRRR.

IF IT'S NOT CLEANING THE BOARD ERASERS, IT'S WATERING THE FLOWERS! IF I SIT NEAR THE WINDOW I'M "WINDOW POLE MONITOR"... IF I'M NEAR THE RADIATOR, I'M "TURNING ON AND OFF THE RADIATOR MONITOR"...

SMACK SMACK SMACK

IT'S GETTING STUFFY IN HERE! ORVILLE, WILL YOU OPEN A WINDOW?

ALWAYS IT'S **ME** THAT'S MONITOR! "CHALK MONITOR", "FILLING EMPTY INK WELLS MONITOR"... SO I GO HOME AND MAMMA SAYS, "YOU GOTTA MAKE HOME DUTIES AS MUCH FUN FOR CHILDREN AS THEIR SCHOOL DUTIES"...

SMACK SMACK

SO NOW I'M "TAKE DOWN THE GARBAGE MONITOR", "PUT ALL THE SILVERWARE ON THE TABLE MONITOR", AND "CLEAN OUT THE VACUUM CLEANER MONITOR"!

SMACK SMACK SMACK

ONE O'THESE DAYS I'M GONNA WALK INTO CLASS AND TELL MISS SLUDGE...

?

ALWAYS, **ALWAYS** THEY PICK ON **ME**!

PRINCIPAL

MARCH 5 1950

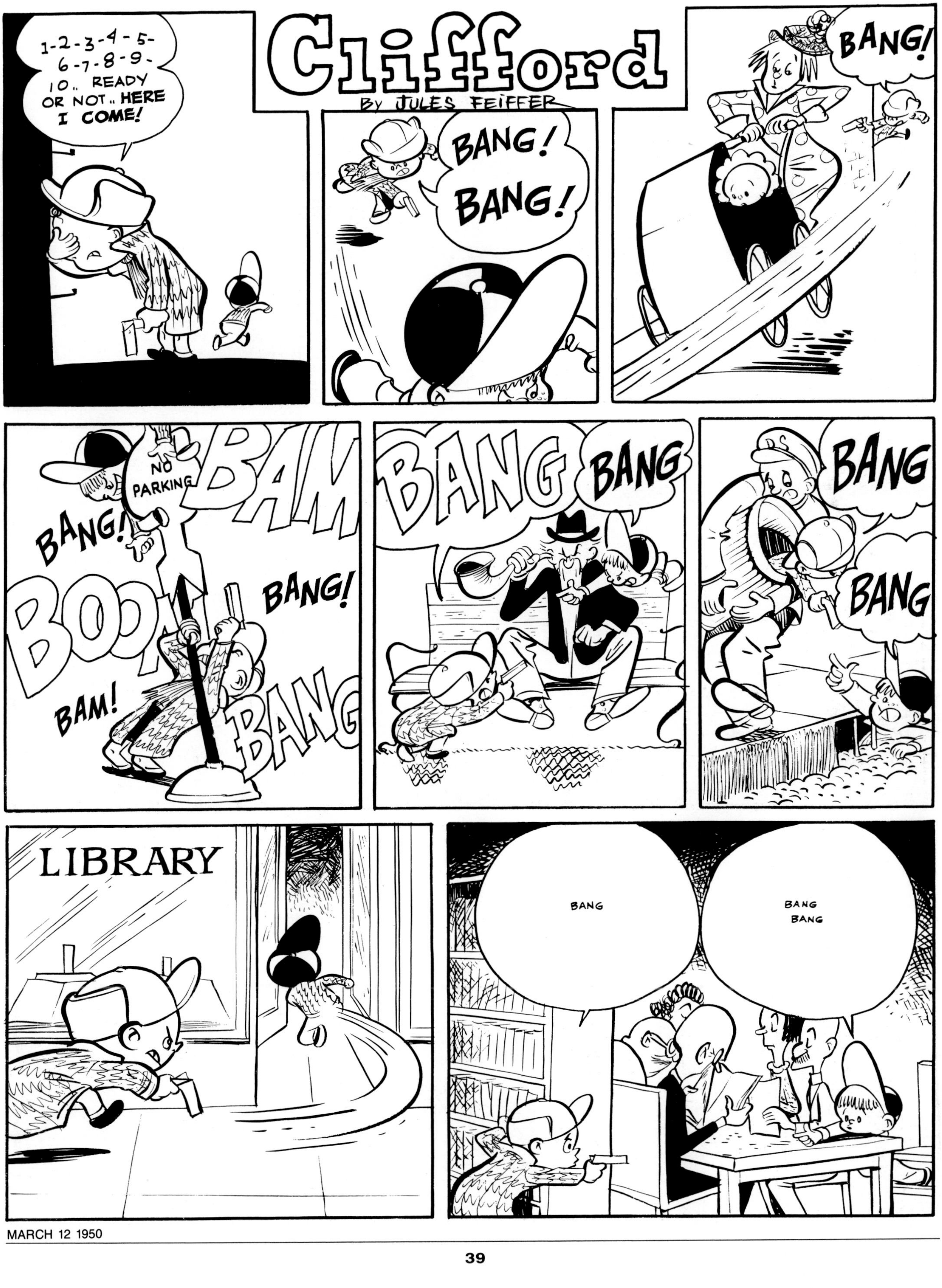
Clifford
By JULES FEIFFER
1-2-3-4-5-6-7-8-9-10.. READY OR NOT.. HERE I COME!
BANG!
BANG!
BANG!
NO PARKING
BAM
BANG!
BOOM
BANG!
BAM!
BANG
BANG
BANG
BANG
BANG
LIBRARY
BANG
BANG
BANG

MARCH 12 1950

Clifford
BY JULES FEIFFER

CREEPALONG HAGGERTY MOVED HIS LONG LEGS DOWN THE WIDE, FRONTIER STREET...

HIS "CREEPALONG HAGGERTY SPECIAL GUN" RESTED EASY-LIKE AGAINST HIS "CREEPALONG HAGGERTY HANDY DANDY CHAPS..."

HIS BODY WAS RELAXED EASY-LIKE, BUT IN HIS EYES BLAZED THE GLINT OF DANGER THAT BORE NO GOOD TO EVIL-DOERS...AND ENEMIES OF THE LAW!

FROM THE OPPOSITE SIDE OF THE LONG AVENUE, WITH HIS "CREEPALONG HAGGERTY CONTACT LENSES," HE COULD SEE HIS ENEMY APPROACHING...

HE MOVED DOWN THE WIDE ROAD WITH AN EASY-LIKE CAUTION... AND STOPPED...AND WAITED...

CREEPALONG HAGGERTY! COME TO SCHOOL... YOU'RE LATE!

WITH HIS "SPECIAL CREEPALONG HAGGERTY LIGHTNING DRAW"... **CREEPY'S GUNS BLAZED INTO HIS HANDS!**

BANG

I DON'T KNOW WHAT'S WRONG WITH THE BOY, SINCE I GOT HIM UP FOR SCHOOL! HE HASN'T SAID A WORD!

SHE OUTDREW CREEPY... SHE EVEN OUTDREW CREEPY...

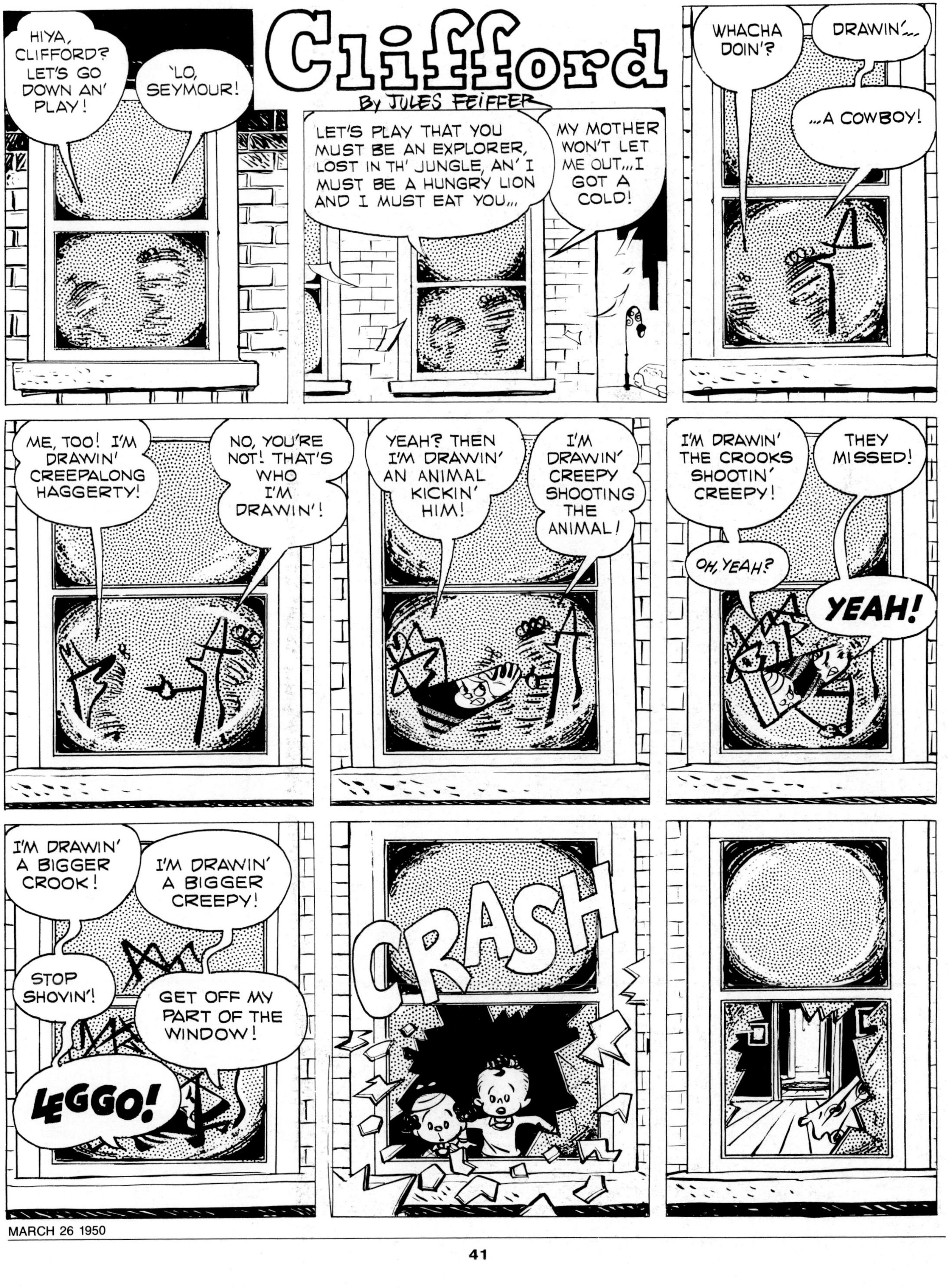
HIYA, CLIFFORD? LET'S GO DOWN AN' PLAY!
'LO, SEYMOUR!
Clifford
By JULES FEIFFER
LET'S PLAY THAT YOU MUST BE AN EXPLORER, LOST IN TH' JUNGLE, AN' I MUST BE A HUNGRY LION AND I MUST EAT YOU...
MY MOTHER WON'T LET ME OUT... I GOT A COLD!
WHACHA DOIN'?
DRAWIN'...
...A COWBOY!
ME, TOO! I'M DRAWIN' CREEPALONG HAGGERTY!
NO, YOU'RE NOT! THAT'S WHO I'M DRAWIN'!
YEAH? THEN I'M DRAWIN' AN ANIMAL KICKIN' HIM!
I'M DRAWIN' CREEPY SHOOTING THE ANIMAL!
I'M DRAWIN' THE CROOKS SHOOTIN' CREEPY!
THEY MISSED!
OH, YEAH?
YEAH!
I'M DRAWIN' A BIGGER CROOK!
I'M DRAWIN' A BIGGER CREEPY!
STOP SHOVIN'!
GET OFF MY PART OF THE WINDOW!
LEGGO!
CRASH

MARCH 26 1950

Clifford
BY JULES FEIFFER

NOW, BE CALM WALDO! THE **LEAST** A PARENT CAN DO IS VISIT HIS CHILDS' CLASS DURING OPEN SCHOOL WEEK! IT'S AN INSTITUTION.... LIKE VOTING.

WELCOME WELCOME **WELCOME!** PARENTS! WE KNOW HOW ANXIOUS YOU ARE TO SEE YOUR CHILD AT WORK--- SO JUST SIT BACK IN THE REAR OF THE ROOM!

GRUMBLE GRUMBLE DARN SEAT IS TIGHT

PARENTS MUST BE QUIET SO THAT THE LESSON MAY CONTINUE.

WILL THE PARENTS PLEASE REMOVE THEIR HATS AND PIPE ---WE MUSTN'T SET BAD EXAMPLES FOR OUR YOUNGSTERS.

WELL CLASS IS OVER FOR TODAY! THANK YOU VERY MUCH FOR COMING.

I CAN'T GO...

I'M STUCK..

BANG BANG BANG

BANG

I'VE NEVER BEEN SO EMBARRASSED IN ALL MY LIFE!

APRIL 2 1950

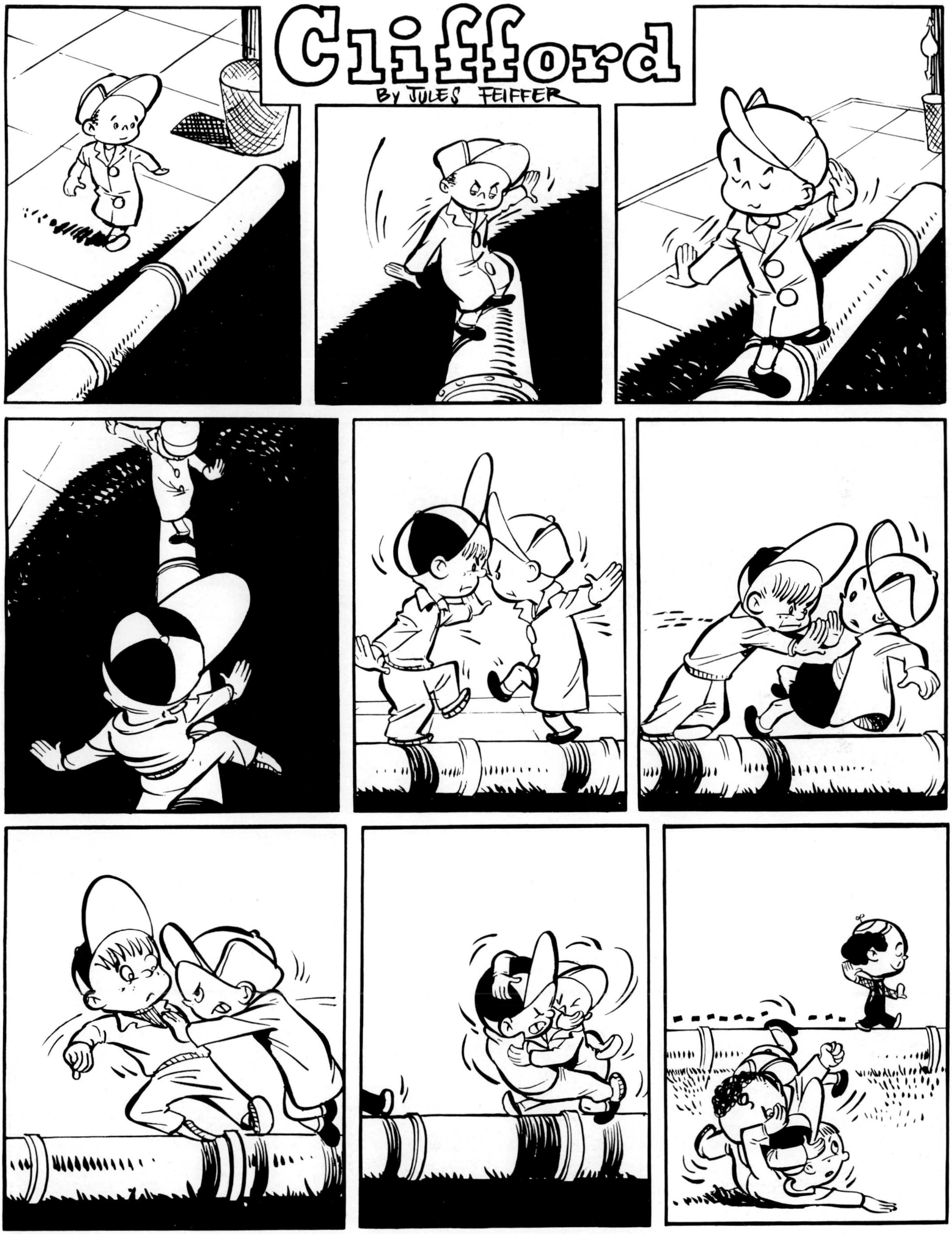
Clifford
BY JULES FEIFFER

APRIL 9 1950

Clifford
BY JULES FEIFFER

APRIL 16 1950

Clifford
BY JULES FEIFFER

PUFF

HERE YOU ARE, LITTLE BOY!

PUFF

Clifford
BY JULES FEIFFER

APRIL 30 1950

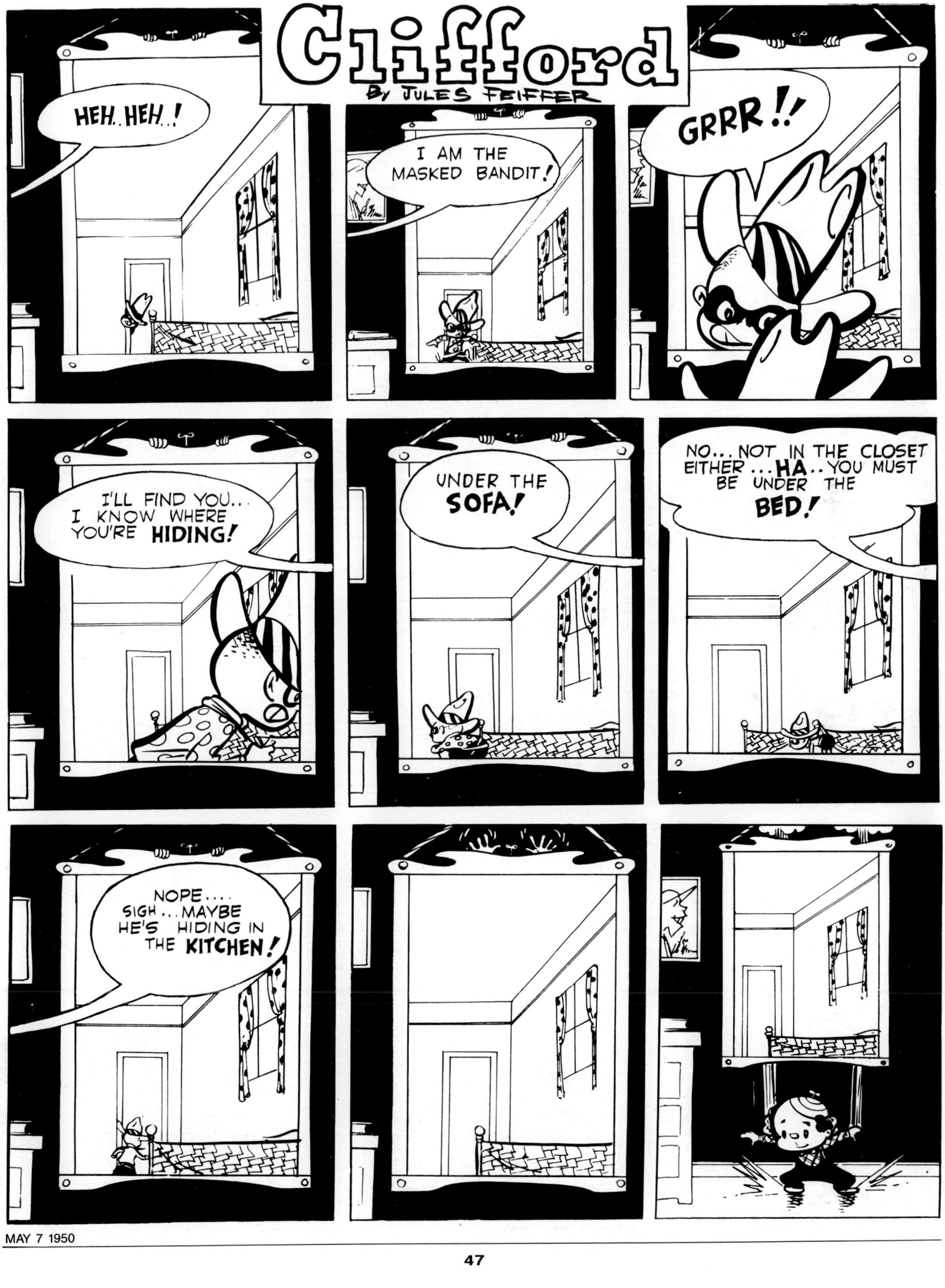
Clifford
BY JULES FEIFFER
HEH..HEH..!
I AM THE MASKED BANDIT!
GRRR!!
I'LL FIND YOU... I KNOW WHERE YOU'RE HIDING!
UNDER THE SOFA!
NO... NOT IN THE CLOSET EITHER ...HA.. YOU MUST BE UNDER THE BED!
NOPE.... SIGH... MAYBE HE'S HIDING IN THE KITCHEN!

MAY 7 1950

Clifford
BY JULES FEIFFER

MAY 14 1950

Clifford

BY JULES FEIFFER

LET'S SAY YOU HAVEN'T DONE YOUR ARITHMETIC HOMEWORK THIS WEEK....

CLIFFORD, ORVILLE AND NATALIE, WILL YOU PLEASE PUT TODAYS ARITHMETIC ON THE BOARD!

THE FIRST THING TO DO IS GO THROUGH YOUR LOOSELEAF BOOK THREE OR FOUR TIMES, LOOKING FOR THE HOMEWORK...

AFTER A COUPLE OF MINUTES OF DOING THIS, SELECT ONE SHEET AT RANDOM AND REMOVE IT FROM THE BOOK...FUMBLING A MINUTE OR SO WITH THE CLAMPS...

WALK VERY SLOWLY TO THE FRONT OF THE ROOM.... TRY STUMBLING...

ONCE UP TO THE BLACKBOARD, HAVE TROUBLE DECIDING WHICH SECTION OF BOARD YOU WANT TO USE...

WRITING YOUR NAME BECOMES A GREAT PROBLEM AND IT MUST BE ERASED A HALF A DOZEN TIMES....DURING WHICH TIME YOU STEP ON ALL THE CHALK AND MUST GO OUT AND GET SOME MORE...

RING!

THAT ENDS CLASS FOR TODAY! GOOD AFTERNOON, CHILDREN!

PHEW! I'LL NEVER NOT DO MY HOMEWORK AGAIN!

MAY 21 1950

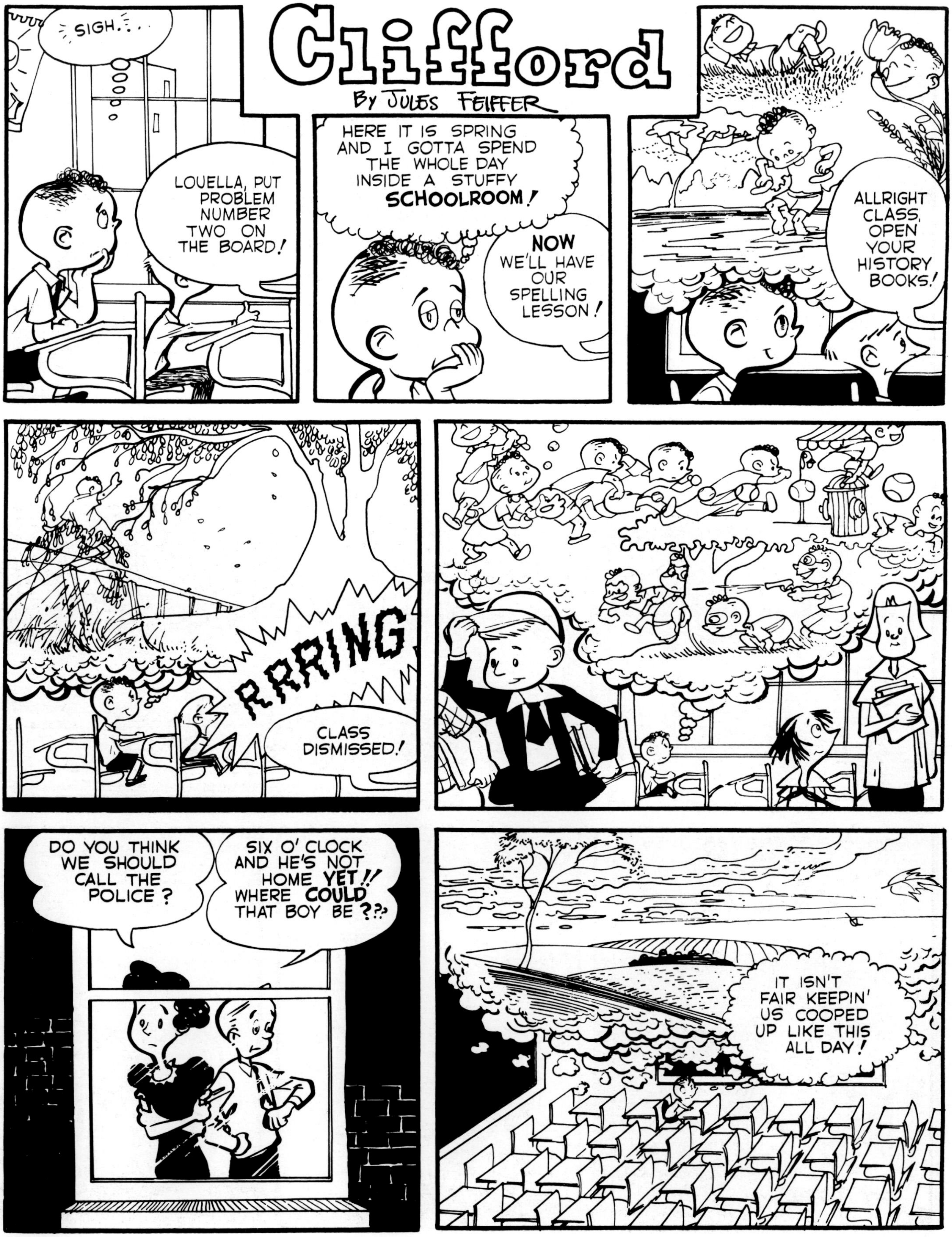
Clifford
By Jules Feiffer
SIGH.
LOUELLA, PUT PROBLEM NUMBER TWO ON THE BOARD!
HERE IT IS SPRING AND I GOTTA SPEND THE WHOLE DAY INSIDE A STUFFY SCHOOLROOM!
NOW WE'LL HAVE OUR SPELLING LESSON!
ALLRIGHT CLASS, OPEN YOUR HISTORY BOOKS!
RRRING
CLASS DISMISSED!
DO YOU THINK WE SHOULD CALL THE POLICE?
SIX O' CLOCK AND HE'S NOT HOME YET!! WHERE COULD THAT BOY BE ??
IT ISN'T FAIR KEEPIN' US COOPED UP LIKE THIS ALL DAY!

MAY 28 1950

Clifford
BY JULES FEIFFER

ON THE AIR

THAT'S MY DADDY UP THERE!

SEE? THAT'S HIM!

MY DADDY!

SHHH...

NOW SIR, YOU HAVE REACHED THE STAGE THAT FEW...FEW OF OUR CONTESTANTS EVER REACH..... **THE JET JACKPOT QUESTION!!!**

THE AIR

WOW!

ANSWER THIS QUESTION CORRECTLY AND YOU WILL RECEIVE **FIVE HUNDRED DOLLARS IN CASH**..... YOU.... HAVE **TEN** SECONDS!

WHO WAS THE SIXTEENTH PRESIDENT OF THE UNITED STATES?

ABRAH...

BOOM BIDDY BOOM BIDDY BOOM BIDDY BOOM

THINK! THINK CAREFULLY.. FOR FIVE HUNDRED DOLLARS DEPENDS ON YOUR ANSWER... YOU HAVE **NINE SECONDS** LEFT.... **EIGHT SECONDS**...

ABRA...

BOOM BIDDY BOOM BIDDY

SEVEN SECONDS... TIME IS FLEETING, MAN! **SIX**...

BOOM BIDDY BOOM BIDDY BOOM

ABR...

BOOM BIDDY BOOM

FIVE·· FOUR·· **THREE**·· $500 IN CASH... WILL HE WIN IT? **TWO**...

BOOM BIDDY BOOM BIDDY BIDDY BIDDY **BOOM** BIDDY

ONE SECOND!.. **BZZZZZz**

I'M **DREAD**FULLY SORRY, SIR, **TIME IS UP!** AS A CONSOLATION, HERE IS A CARTON OF OUR SPONSORS PRODUCT, HOOPERDUNKELS CAVITY FILLINGS!.. BETTER LUCK NEXT TIME!

BZZT BOOM CLANG CLANG RAT TAT BOOM BIDDY

IF Y'HAD ONLY LOOKED AT ME... IT WAS ABRAHAM LINCOLN.. I KNEW THE ANSWER ...I WUZ MOTIONIN' TO YA.. YA SHOULDA LOOKED..

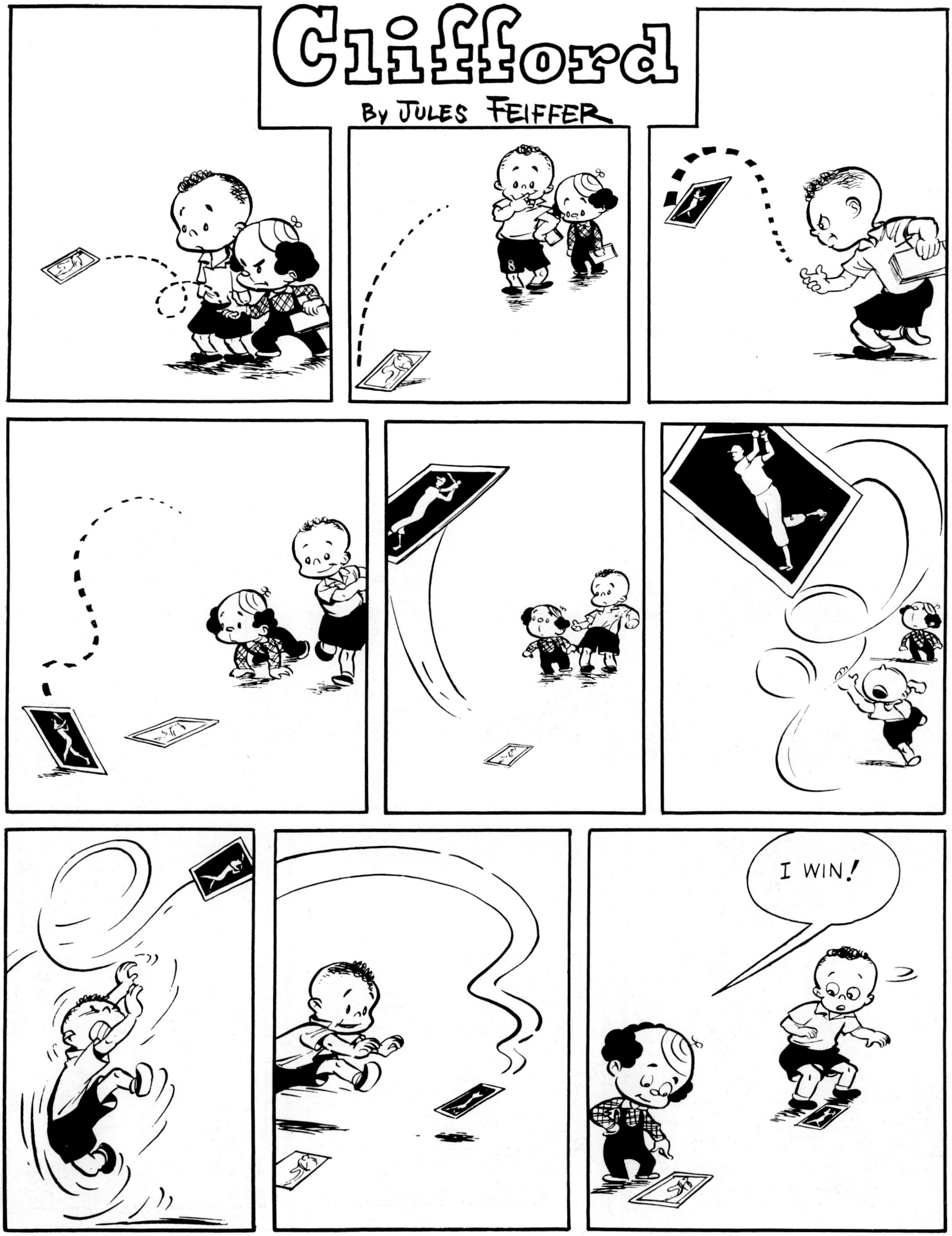
Clifford
By JULES FEIFFER
I WIN!

JUNE 11 1950

Clifford

By Jules Feiffer

THERE'S A **TREMENDOUS** CROWD OUT HERE T'DAY FOLKS...THE OFFICIAL ATTENDANCE FIGURES AREN'T IN YET, BUT IT'S A **LARGE** TURNOUT...

THERE'S AN EXPECTANT HUSH OVER THE CROWD....THEY'RE ALL LOOKING TOWARD THE... ...WAIT....HERE HE COMES .....CLIFFORD!

EASILY HE CLUTCHES THE MARBLES AS HE MAKES THE **LONG** TRIP ACROSS THE STREET....

HE'S ON THE MARK NOW... RUBS HIS MARBLE BAG... SCOWLS AT THE CHEESE BOX...HE'S **READY**...

HE POISES THE REELY ON THE EDGE OF HIS FOREFINGER...HIS THUMB UP, HIS PINKY DOWN....**HE'S INTO THE WIND UP**...

HEY LOOK!! THE MERRY GO ROUND!

JUNE 18 1950

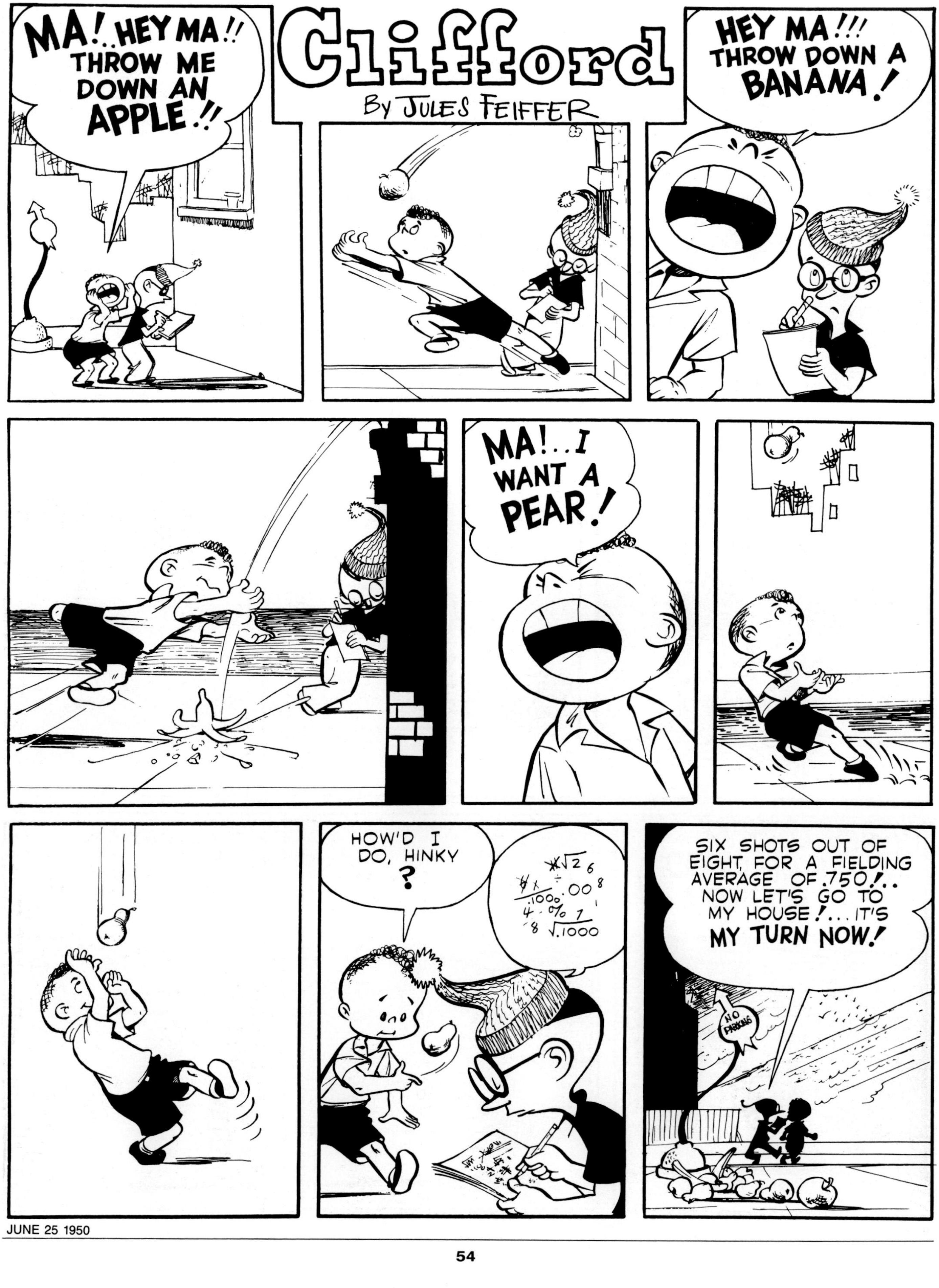
MA!..HEY MA!! THROW ME DOWN AN APPLE!!
Clifford
By JULES FEIFFER
HEY MA!!! THROW DOWN A BANANA!
MA!..I WANT A PEAR!
HOW'D I DO, HINKY?
SIX SHOTS OUT OF EIGHT, FOR A FIELDING AVERAGE OF .750!.. NOW LET'S GO TO MY HOUSE!... IT'S MY TURN NOW!
NO PARKING

JUNE 25 1950

Clifford

BY JULES FEIFFER

JULY 2 1950

HANDY HINTS for CHILDREN

number 2

on going away for the summer

Clifford
BY JULES FEIFFER

LET'S SAY YOU ARE ABOUT TO GO AWAY TO THE COUNTRY FOR THE SUMMER-TIME...

I'M GOIN' AWAY TO THE COUNTRY FOR THE SUMMER-TIME.

EVEN THOUGH YOU ARE YOUNG, YOU MUST OBEY THE SIMPLE RULES OF ETIQUETTE...... POLITELY SAY GOOD-BYE TO YOUR FRIENDS.

I'M GOIN' AWAY TO THE COUNTRY FOR THE SUMMER-TIME!

BID FAREWELL TO ALL, IN A SPIRIT OF GOOD CHEER.

I'M GOIN' AWAY TO THE COUNTRY FOR THE SUMMERTIME.

THEY WILL BE HAPPY FOR YOU...

I'M GOIN' AWAY TO THE COUNTRY FOR THE SUMMERTIME!

DO YOUR BEST TO LIGHTEN THE BURDEN OF YOUR LESS FORTU-NATE HUMAN BEINGS....

I'M GOIN' AWAY TO THE COUNTRY FOR THE SUMMER-TIME!

AND NO MATTER HOW LITTLE IMPORTANCE YOU ATTACH TO YOUR DEEDS...

AS YOU LEAVE, YOU WILL FIND EVIDENT THE DEEP AFFECTION YOU HAVE KINDLED IN THE HEARTS OF YOUR NEIGHBORS.

ARE WE IN THE COUNTRY YET?

JULY 9 1950

Clifford

BY JULES FEIFFER

I **HATE** THOSE MAGAZINE ARTICLES THAT SAY IT'S BETTER TO RAISE A DOG IN THE **COUNTRY** THAN THE **CITY**.

WE **CITY** DOGS ARE MORE AWAKE TO THE **HARSH** REALITIES OF LIFE

SO WHAT, IF WE DON'T HAVE TREES AND GRASS... WE HAVE **OTHER** THINGS..

WE HAVE **MUCH** MORE COMPANIONSHIP.

AND AS FOR SPORT...WHY THE **KEENEST** COUNTRY DOG DOESN'T HAVE THE **COMPETITIVE** INSTINCT OF WE **CITY** DOGS.!

WE CAN EVEN HAVE AS MUCH PRIVACY AS ANY OLD COUNTRY DOG....ALL WE HAVE TO DO IS GO UP ON ANY ROOF AND WE CAN BE **COMPLETELY** ALONE.!

!

Clifford
BY JULES FEIFFER

A...MY NAME IS **ANNA** AND MY SISTER'S NAME IS **ALICE** AND WE LIVE ♪ ON **AMES** STREET ♪

B...MY NAME IS **BETTY** AND MY SISTER'S NAME IS **BARBERA** AND WE LIVE ON **BANK** STREET

AND SO IT GOES....

E...MY NAME IS **ELAINE** AND MY SISTER'S NAME IS **EVA** AND WE LIVE ON **EDEN** STREET ♪

F...G...H...I..........

J... MY NAME IS **JANICE** AND MY SISTER'S NAME IS **JANE** AND WE LIVE ON **JUNE** STREET!

K...L...M...N...O..........

P... MY NAME IS **PAULA** AND SISTER'S NAME IS **PAULETTE** AND WE LIVE ON **PINK** STREET

Q...R...S...T...U..........

V...MY NAME IS...**VALERIE** AND MY SISTER'S NAME IS **VELMA** AND WE LIVE ON.....**VIOLET** STREET ♪

W...AND THEN...

X...MY NAME IS....

IS....

-SIGH-

I...I THOUGHT MAYBE **SHE'D** BE THE **ONE!**

SOMEDAY SOMEBODY WILL DO IT!

JULY 23 1950

Clifford
By Jules Feiffer

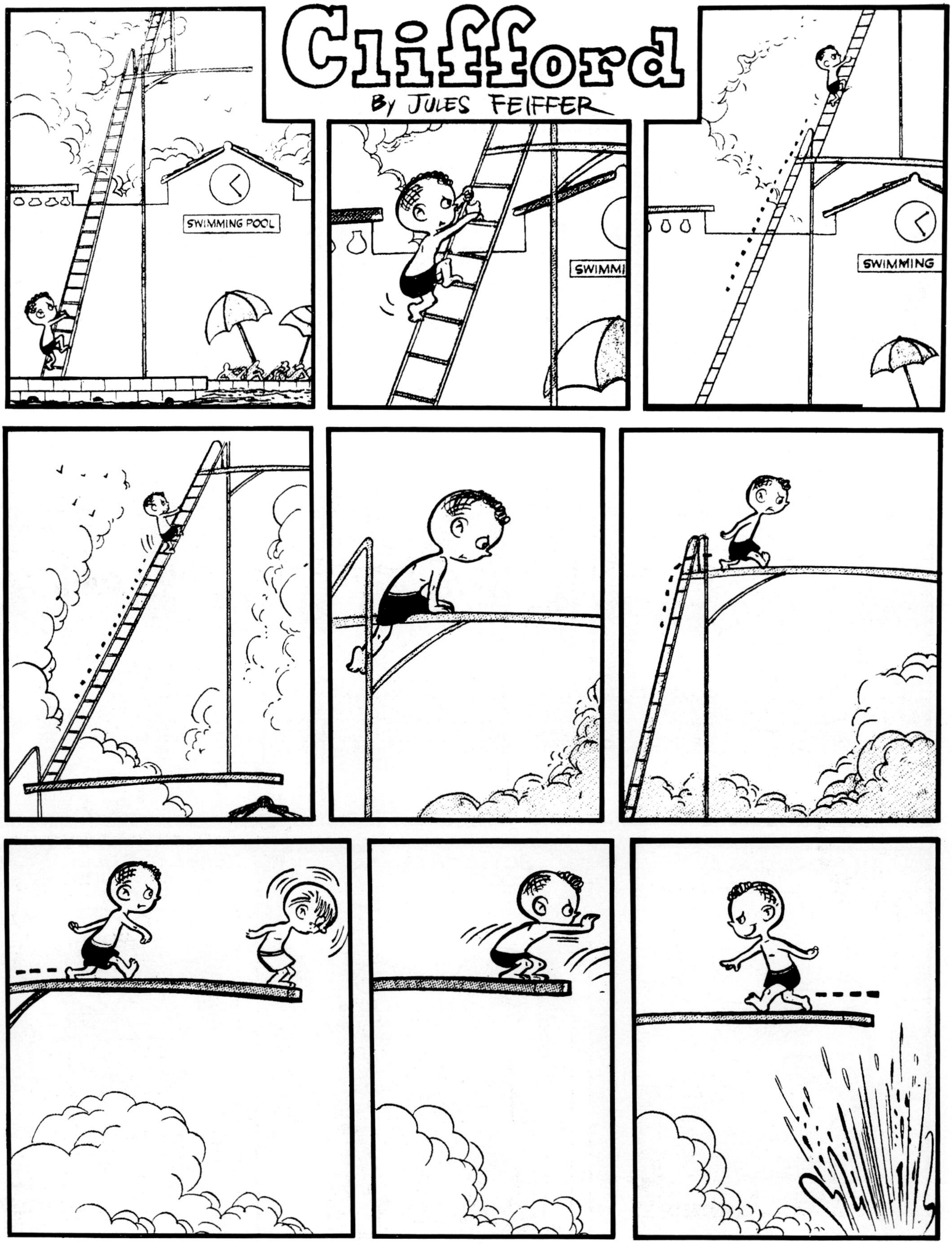
Clifford
By JULES FEIFFER
SWIMMING POOL
SWIMMI
SWIMMING

AUGUST 6 1950

Clifford
BY JULES FEIFFER

IT'S THE LAST OF THE TENTH INNING, THE SCORE IS STILL TIED 0-0, AND THUS FAR NEITHER PITCHER HAS ALLOWED A BASE HIT.'

THE MEAT PART OF THE RED HOSE BATTING ORDER IS COMING UP.....LISTEN TO THE CROWD ROAR.'
RAHHHH...

YES SIR, FANS, THEY'RE ROARING JUST LIKE SMOKERS ALL OVER THE COUNTRY ARE ROARING FOR "SMUDGIES"

Y'KNOW "SMUDGIES" IS THAT RARE BLEND OF EXTRA MILD IMPORTED OUTER MONGOLIAN TOBACCOS THAT HAVE BEEN AGED FOR YEARS IN SUBTERRANEAN CAVERNS TO KEEP THEM FROM GETTING "SUN ROT"
WACK! RAHHHH...

YOUR THROAT WILL BE FREE OF DRYNESS WITH THE EXCLUSIVE NEW "SMUDGIE" AIR VENT FILTER SYSTEM
WHACK! RAHHH...

"AIR VENT FILTERS" ARE THE MANY MINUTE PERFORATIONS BETWEEN EACH INDIVIDUAL GRAIN THAT BRINGS FRESH AIR INTO YOUR LUNGS WITH EVERY PUFF....
WACK! RAHHH...

SO FANS, WHY NOT GO OUT AND BUY "SMUDGIES"...THE SMOKE OF **BIG LEAGUERS** EVERYWHERE.'
WHACK! RAHHHH

AND NOW BACK TO THE BALL GA ??? ☀ SAY..... EVERYBODY SEEMS TO HAVE LEFT THE FIELD...THE GAME MUST BE OVER.'
IF...YOU'LL...JUST...WAIT...A MINUTE...I'LL...FIND...OUT ...WHAT...HAPPENED..

HA HA HA THIS IS REALLY QUITE EMBARRASSING... PHWEET HEY COACH.' HEY....

AUGUST 13 1950

HINTS FOR A
YOUNG BALL PLAYER
NUMBER ONE
FIELDING YOUR POSITION

Clifford
BY JULES FEIFFER

A GOOD FIELDER'S ALWAYS GOTTA BE A STEP AHEAD OF THE BATTER!

LET'S SEE....THERE'S A MAN ON FIRST AND THE TEAM SLUGGER IS UP....

HE USUALLY HITS STRAIGHT AWAY, BUT HIS FEET ARE SHIFTED TOWARD LEFT, WHICH MEANS HE'S GOING TO TRY AND PULL THE BALL TOWARD THE GAP IN LEFT CENTER...

THE WIND IS BLOWIN' SOUTH SOUTHEAST AWAY FROM HOME PLATE WHICH SHOULD CARRY A FLYBALL OUT ABOUT **HERE!**

I'LL PRETEND TO DROP THE BALL, AN' GET THE RUNNER T'BREAK FOR SECOND....

THEN I'LL **RIFLE** IN MY LIGHTNIN' THROW TO SECOND AND DOUBLE HIM UP.....THEN I'LL COME UP TO BAT AN' HIT A HOMERUN...THEN I'LL...

CLIFFORD! COME HOME FOR SUPPER!!

AUGUST 20 1950

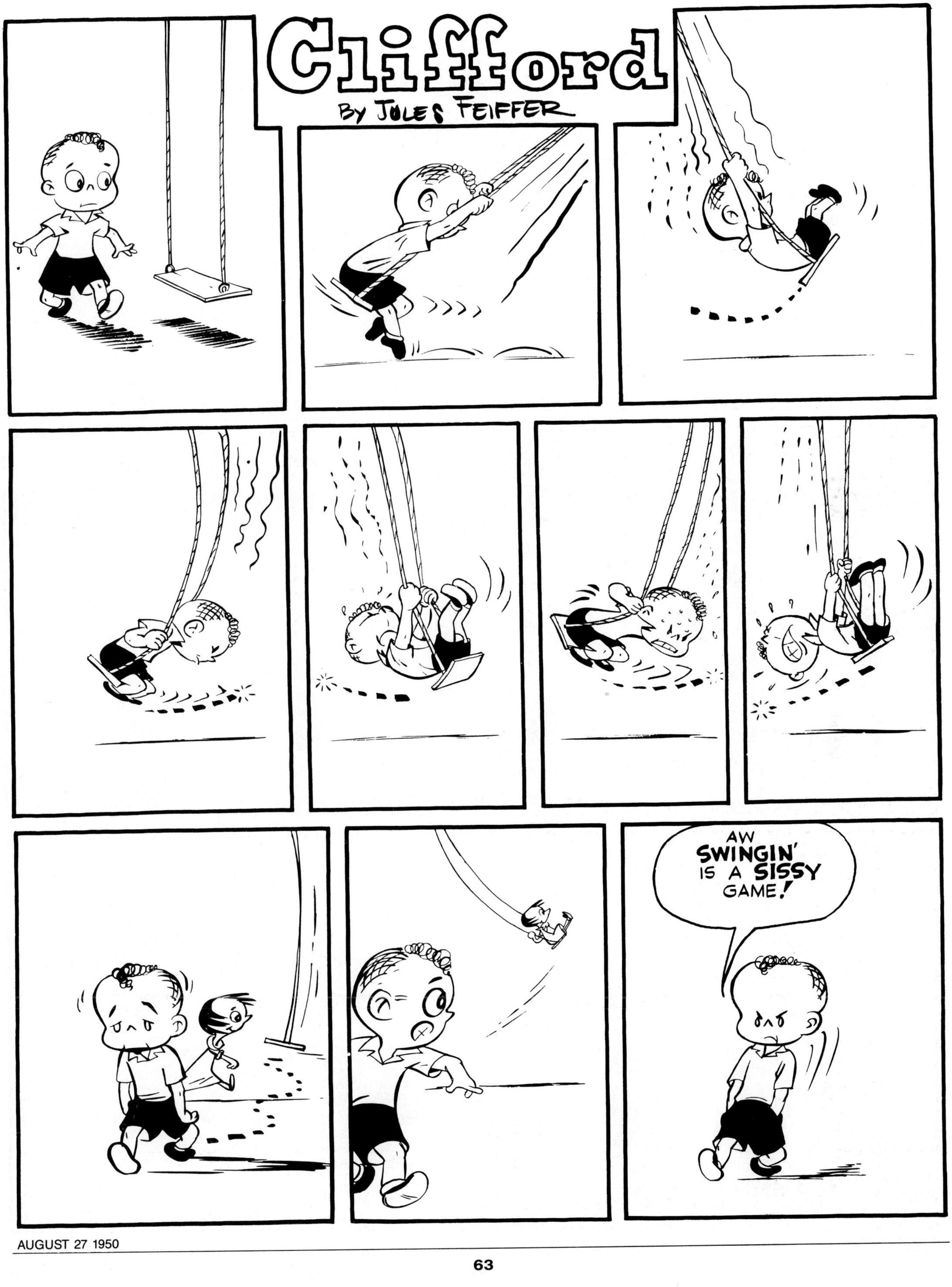
Clifford
By Jules Feiffer
AW SWINGIN' IS A SISSY GAME!

AUGUST 27 1950

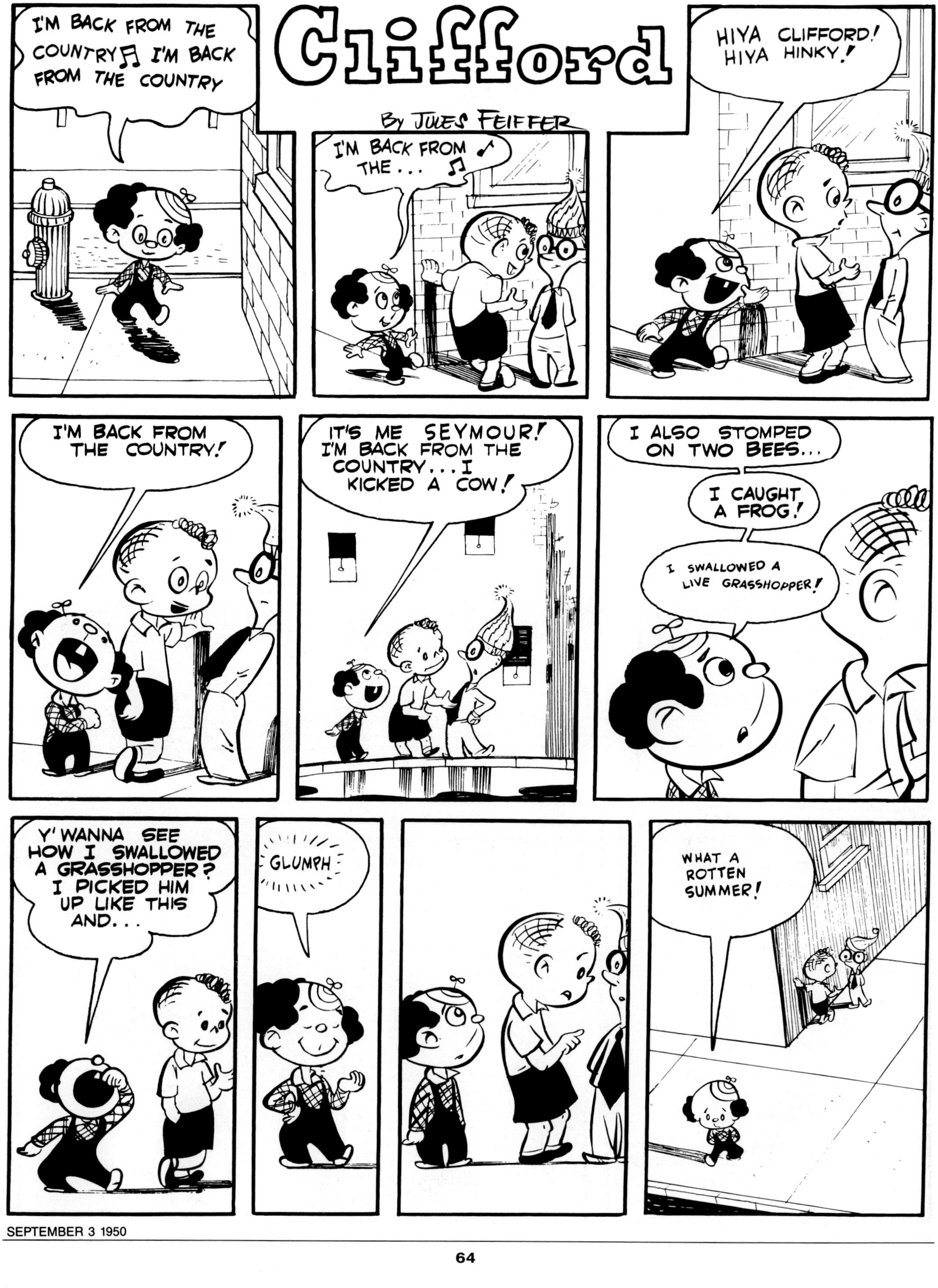
Clifford
By Jules Feiffer
I'M BACK FROM THE COUNTRY I'M BACK FROM THE COUNTRY
I'M BACK FROM THE...
HIYA CLIFFORD! HIYA HINKY!
I'M BACK FROM THE COUNTRY!
IT'S ME SEYMOUR! I'M BACK FROM THE COUNTRY...I KICKED A COW!
I ALSO STOMPED ON TWO BEES...
I CAUGHT A FROG!
I SWALLOWED A LIVE GRASSHOPPER!
Y' WANNA SEE HOW I SWALLOWED A GRASSHOPPER? I PICKED HIM UP LIKE THIS AND...
GLUMPH
WHAT A ROTTEN SUMMER!

SEPTEMBER 3 1950

Clifford

BY JULES FEIFFER

JIMMY HACKNEY IN GANGSTERS REVENGE

JIMMY HACKNEY WALKED INTO THE BACK ROOM... **THIS** WAS TO BE THE SHOWDOWN...

"CROSS ME UP, EH", SNARLED JIMMY HACKNEY ...HE DID NOT NOTICE THE FORTY MACHINE GUNS BEHIND HIM...

JIMMY HACKNEY WHIRLED.. NINETEEN BULLETS TORE THROUGH HIS HEART...

SERIOUSLY WOUNDED, HE STAGGERED DOWN THE BLOCK AND UP THE CHURCH STEPS....

SUDDENLY, PRISCILLA HELD HIM IN HER ARMS, HER HOT TEARS STAINED HIS NECKTIE...

"GO BACK TO THAT YOUNG ENGLISH TEACHER", MUTTERED JIMMY HACKNEY, "I WAS NEVER ANY GOOD FOR YA". HIS HEAD DROOPED..... JIMMY HACKNEY WAS DEAD...

Clifford

BY JULES FEIFFER

SEPTEMBER 17 1950

Clifford
BY JULES FEIFFER

CLIFFORD, WILL YOU PLEASE COME UP HERE AND RECITE TODAY'S POEM!

AHEM!

THE VILLAGE BLACKSMITH BY HENRY WADSWORTH LONGFELLOW!

UNDER A SPREADING CHESTNUT TREE THE VILLAGE SMITHY STANDS...

HMM

SAY, INSTEAD OF ALL THIS, HOW ABOUT A COUPLE OF CUTE SONGS I HEARD THE OTHER NIGHT?

AND SO, ALL THAT AFTERNOON...

SEPTEMBER 24 1950

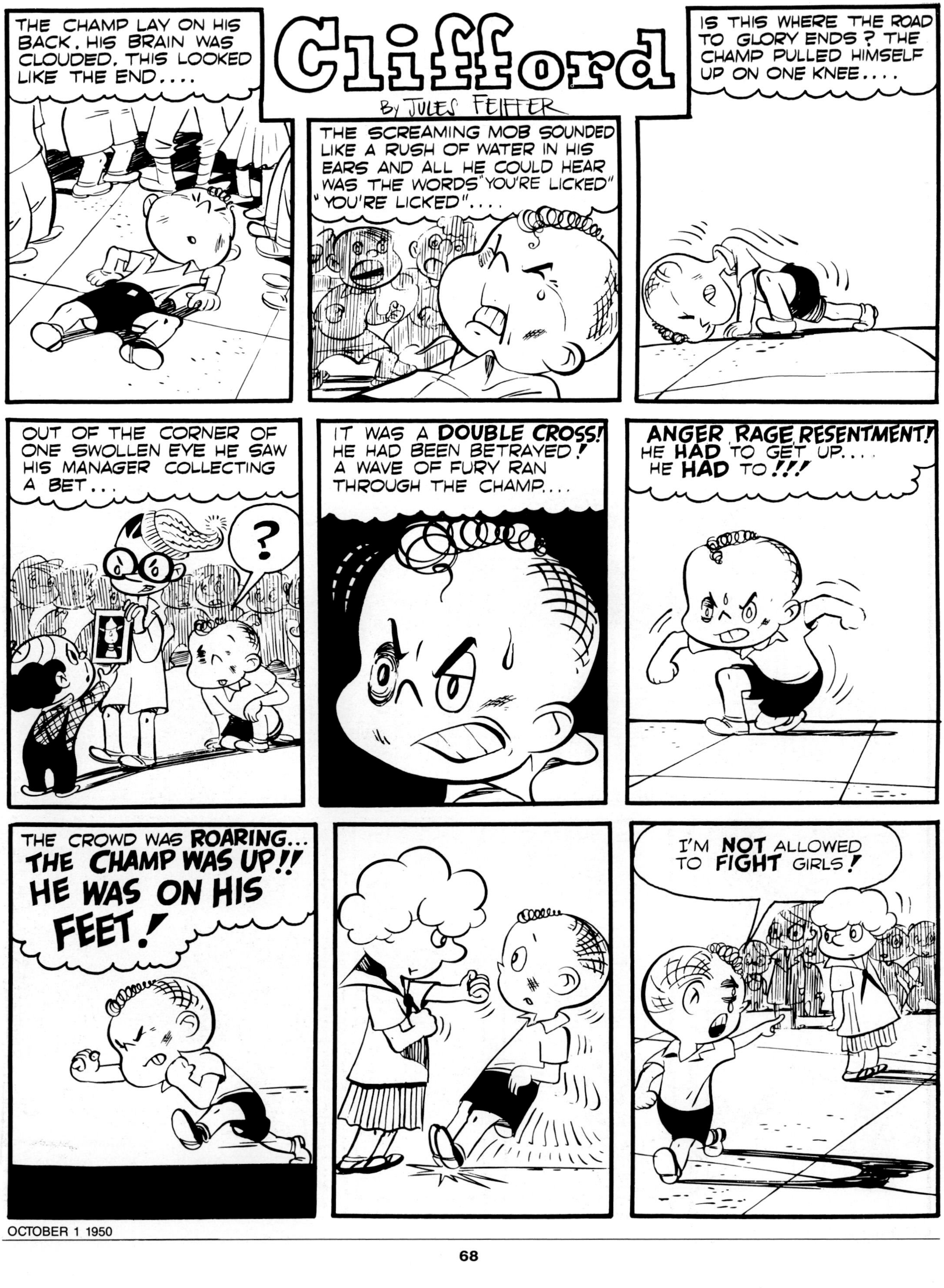
Clifford
By JULES FEIFFER
THE CHAMP LAY ON HIS BACK. HIS BRAIN WAS CLOUDED. THIS LOOKED LIKE THE END....
THE SCREAMING MOB SOUNDED LIKE A RUSH OF WATER IN HIS EARS AND ALL HE COULD HEAR WAS THE WORDS "YOU'RE LICKED" "YOU'RE LICKED"....
IS THIS WHERE THE ROAD TO GLORY ENDS? THE CHAMP PULLED HIMSELF UP ON ONE KNEE....
OUT OF THE CORNER OF ONE SWOLLEN EYE HE SAW HIS MANAGER COLLECTING A BET...
?
IT WAS A DOUBLE CROSS! HE HAD BEEN BETRAYED! A WAVE OF FURY RAN THROUGH THE CHAMP....
ANGER, RAGE, RESENTMENT! HE HAD TO GET UP.... HE HAD TO!!!
THE CROWD WAS ROARING... THE CHAMP WAS UP!! HE WAS ON HIS FEET!
I'M NOT ALLOWED TO FIGHT GIRLS!

OCTOBER 1 1950

Clifford

BY JULES FEIFFER

OCTOBER 8 1950

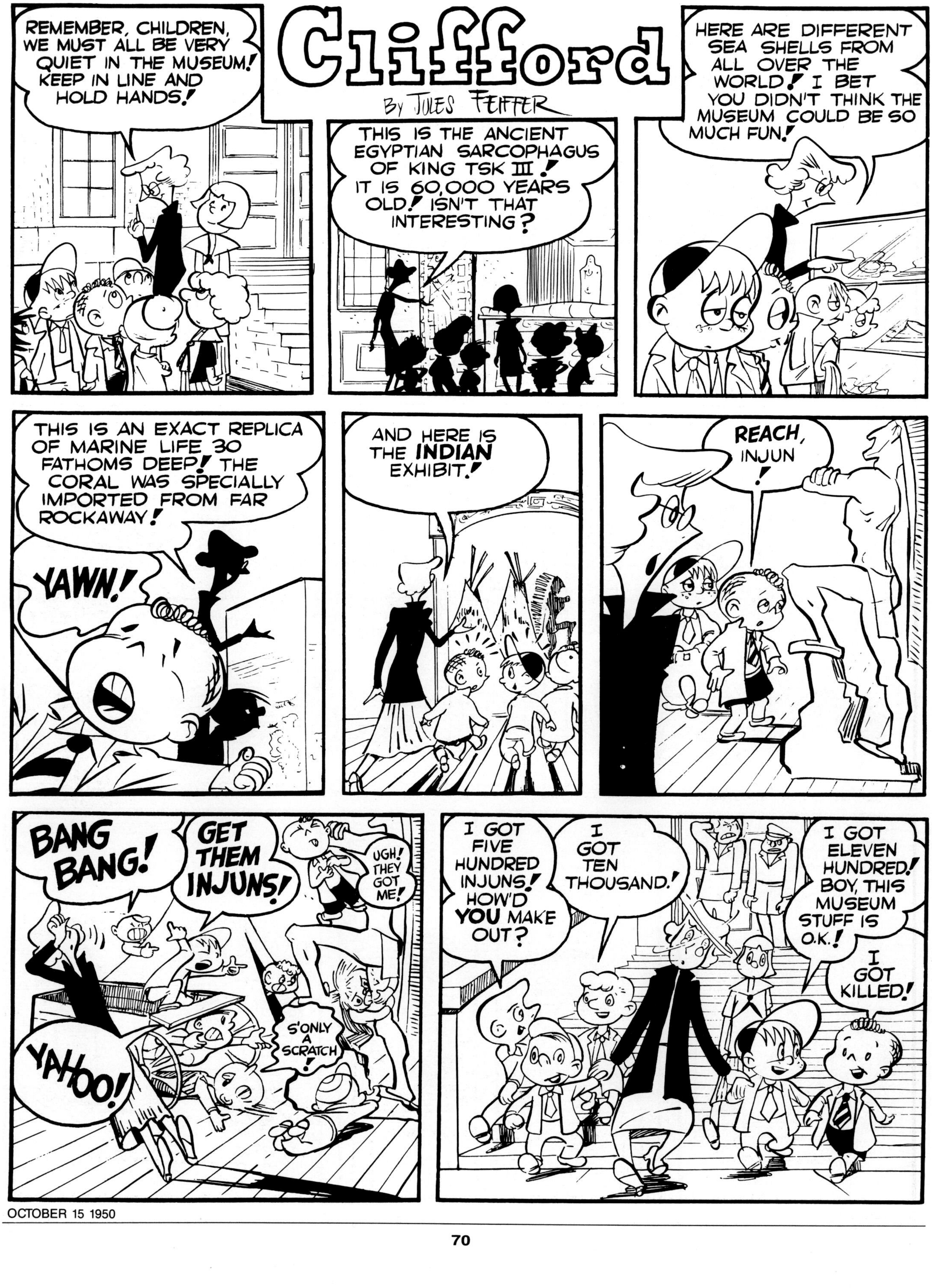
Clifford
By Jules Feiffer
REMEMBER, CHILDREN, WE MUST ALL BE VERY QUIET IN THE MUSEUM! KEEP IN LINE AND HOLD HANDS!
THIS IS THE ANCIENT EGYPTIAN SARCOPHAGUS OF KING TSK III! IT IS 60,000 YEARS OLD! ISN'T THAT INTERESTING?
HERE ARE DIFFERENT SEA SHELLS FROM ALL OVER THE WORLD! I BET YOU DIDN'T THINK THE MUSEUM COULD BE SO MUCH FUN!
THIS IS AN EXACT REPLICA OF MARINE LIFE 30 FATHOMS DEEP! THE CORAL WAS SPECIALLY IMPORTED FROM FAR ROCKAWAY!
YAWN!
AND HERE IS THE INDIAN EXHIBIT!
REACH, INJUN!
BANG BANG!
GET THEM INJUNS!
UGH! THEY GOT ME!
YAHOO!
S'ONLY A SCRATCH!
I GOT FIVE HUNDRED INJUNS! HOW'D YOU MAKE OUT?
I GOT TEN THOUSAND.
I GOT ELEVEN HUNDRED! BOY, THIS MUSEUM STUFF IS O.K.!
I GOT KILLED!

OCTOBER 15 1950

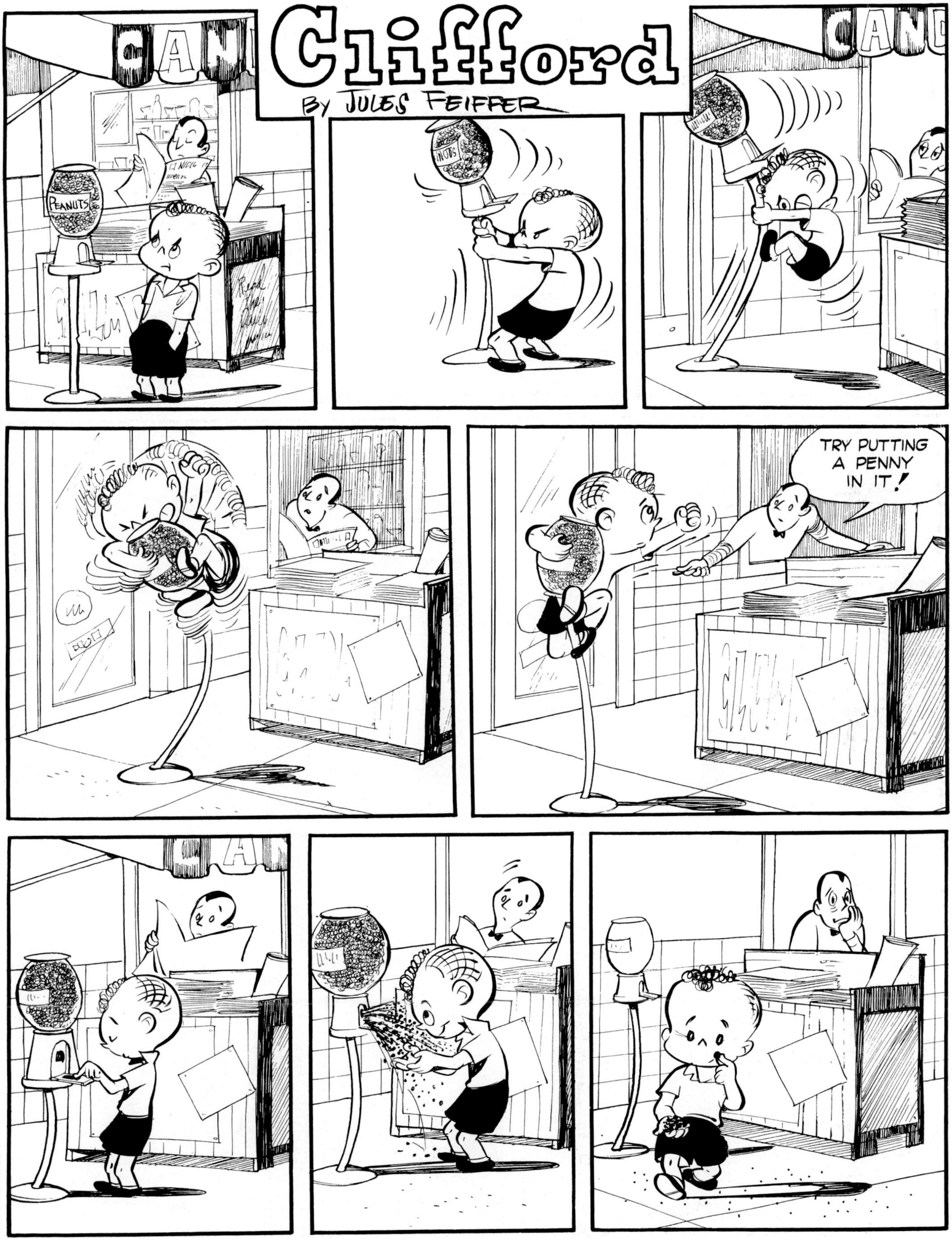
Clifford
By Jules Feiffer
CAND
PEANUTS
TRY PUTTING A PENNY IN IT!

OCTOBER 22 1950

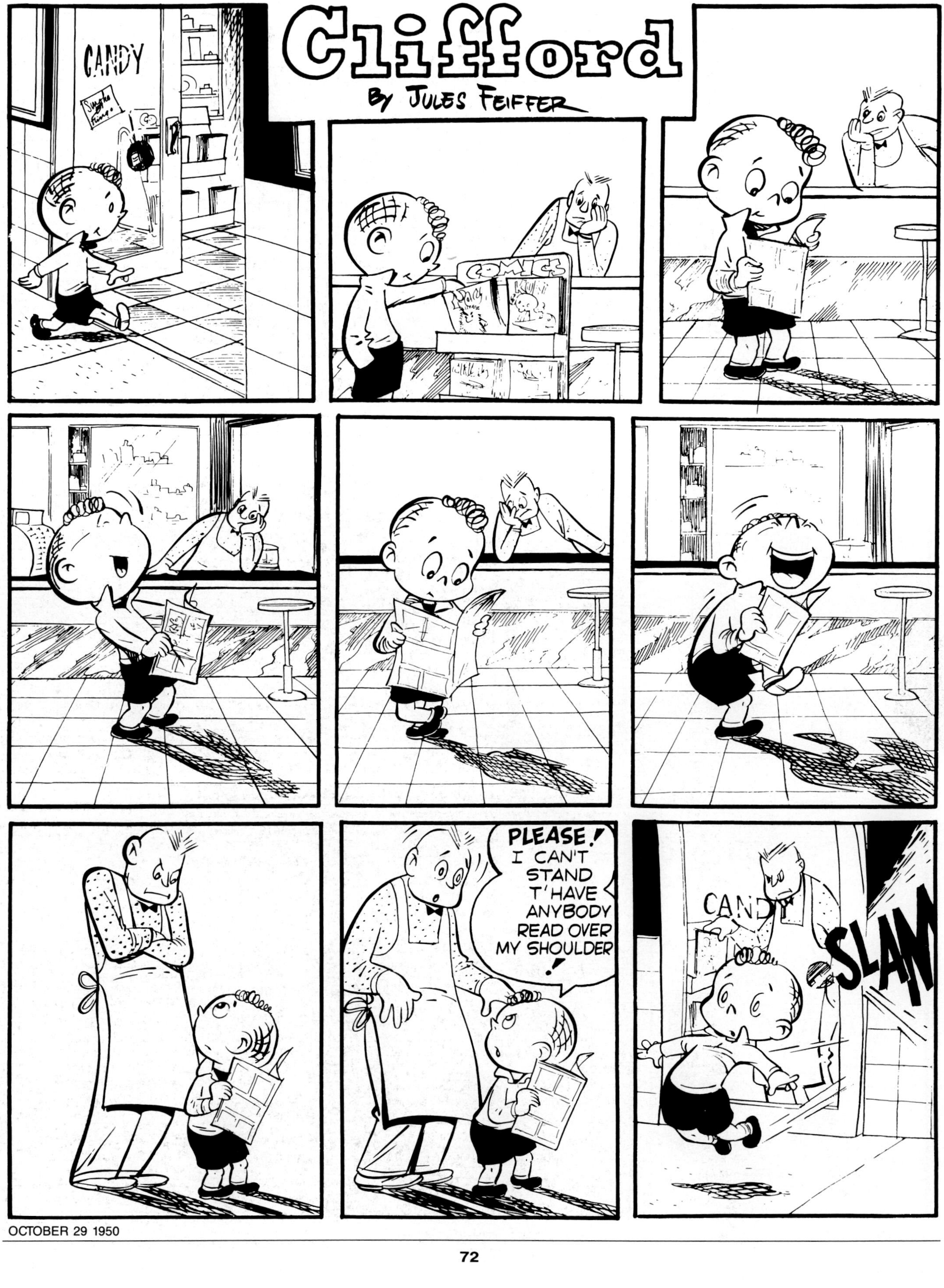
Clifford
By Jules Feiffer
CANDY
COMICS
PLEASE! I CAN'T STAND T'HAVE ANYBODY READ OVER MY SHOULDER!
CANDY
SLAM

OCTOBER 29 1950

Clifford

BY JULES FEIFFER

LAST STOP! ALL OUT!

SCREECHHHHH

NEXT TIME I'LL TAKE A TAXI!

THANKS, POP!

NOVEMBER 5 1950

Clifford

BY JULES FEIFFER

A **BULLFIGHTER!** THAT'S WHAT **I'M** GONNA BE WHEN I GROW UP!

the BULL FIGHT

NOW SHOWING

I CAN SEE ME NOW, STANDING IN THE ARENA, FLOWERS AT MY FEET, BOWING TO THE LADIES!

YEAH? I BET Y' CAN'T GUESS WHAT **I'M** GONNA BE!

THE HORNS BLOW, THE CROWD CHEERS AND OUT COMES THE BULL!

GO AHEAD! I'LL GIVE YA **THREE** GUESSES!

HE SEES ME. HE PAWS THE GROUND. PROUDLY I FLICK MY CAPE...

FOUR GUESSES?

THE BULL CHARGES! I LIGHTLY STEP ASIDE!

SIX GUESSES?

AGAIN HE CHARGES.!! I STAND THERE NOT MOVIN' AN INCH, MY SWORD OUT, AIMED AT A VITAL SPOT ON HIS FOREHEAD!

DON'T GUESS... I'LL TELL YA!

GAAAᴀᴀ!

HE... HE'S GOT ME. I FALL GRACE-FULLY TO THE GROUND, ..A ROSE IS THROWN UPON MY CHEST... THERE ARE TEARS IN THE EYES OF THE CROWD! **I AM DEAD.!!**

THAT'S WHAT **I'M** GONNA BE! NOW TELL ME SEYMOUR, WHAT WAS IT THAT **YOU** WANTED TO BE?

THE BULL!

NOVEMBER 12 1950

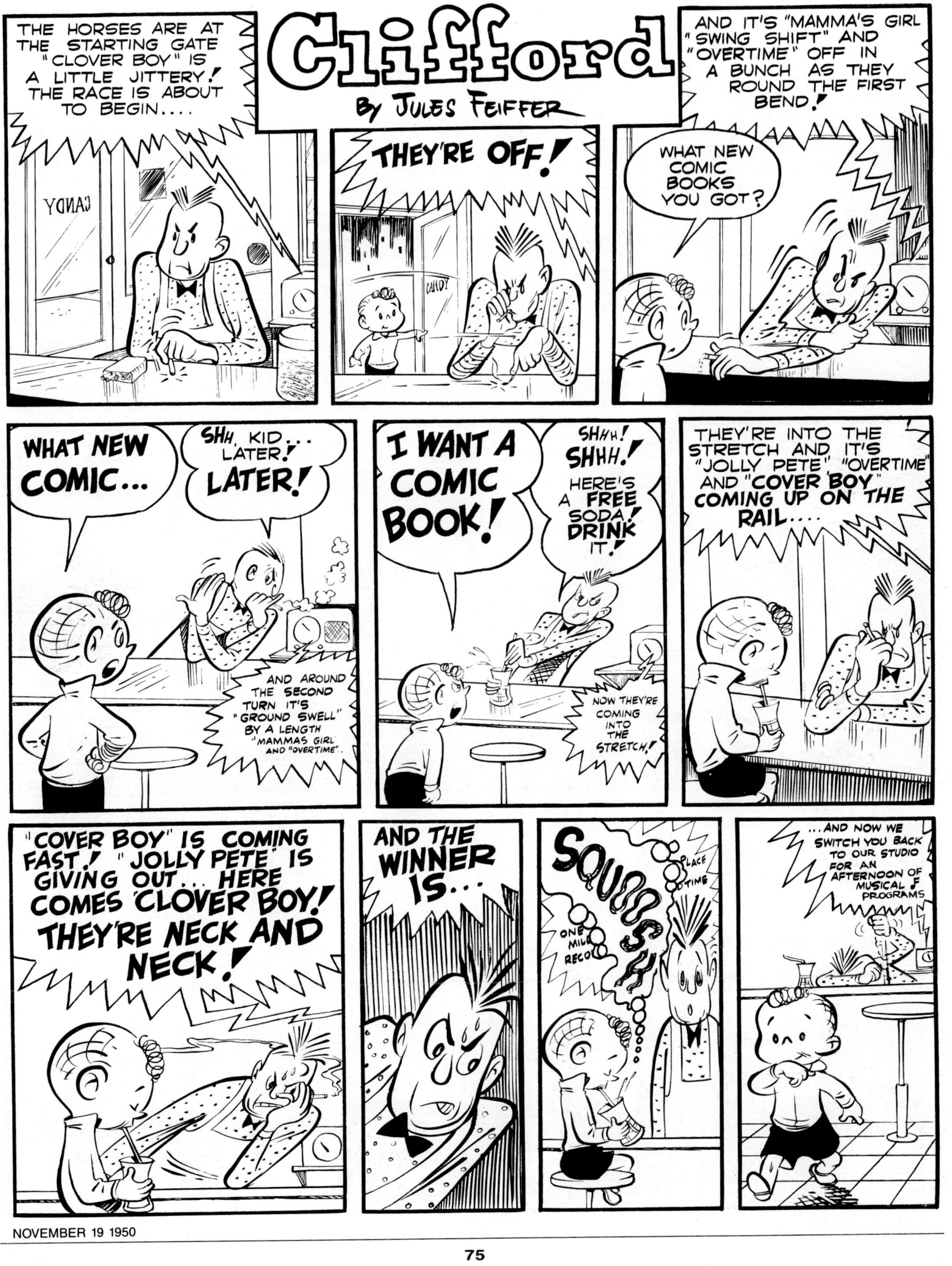
THE HORSES ARE AT THE STARTING GATE "CLOVER BOY" IS A LITTLE JITTERY! THE RACE IS ABOUT TO BEGIN....
Clifford
By Jules Feiffer
THEY'RE OFF!
AND IT'S "MAMMA'S GIRL" "SWING SHIFT" AND "OVERTIME" OFF IN A BUNCH AS THEY ROUND THE FIRST BEND!
WHAT NEW COMIC BOOKS YOU GOT?
WHAT NEW COMIC...
SHH, KID... LATER! LATER!
AND AROUND THE SECOND TURN IT'S "GROUND SWELL" BY A LENGTH "MAMMAS GIRL" AND "OVERTIME".
I WANT A COMIC BOOK!
SHHH! SHHH! HERE'S A FREE SODA! DRINK IT!
NOW THEY'RE COMING INTO THE STRETCH!
THEY'RE INTO THE STRETCH AND IT'S "JOLLY PETE", "OVERTIME" AND "COVER BOY" COMING UP ON THE RAIL....
"COVER BOY" IS COMING FAST! "JOLLY PETE" IS GIVING OUT... HERE COMES 'CLOVER BOY'! THEY'RE NECK AND NECK!
AND THE WINNER IS...
...AND NOW WE SWITCH YOU BACK TO OUR STUDIO FOR AN AFTERNOON OF MUSICAL PROGRAMS

NOVEMBER 19 1950

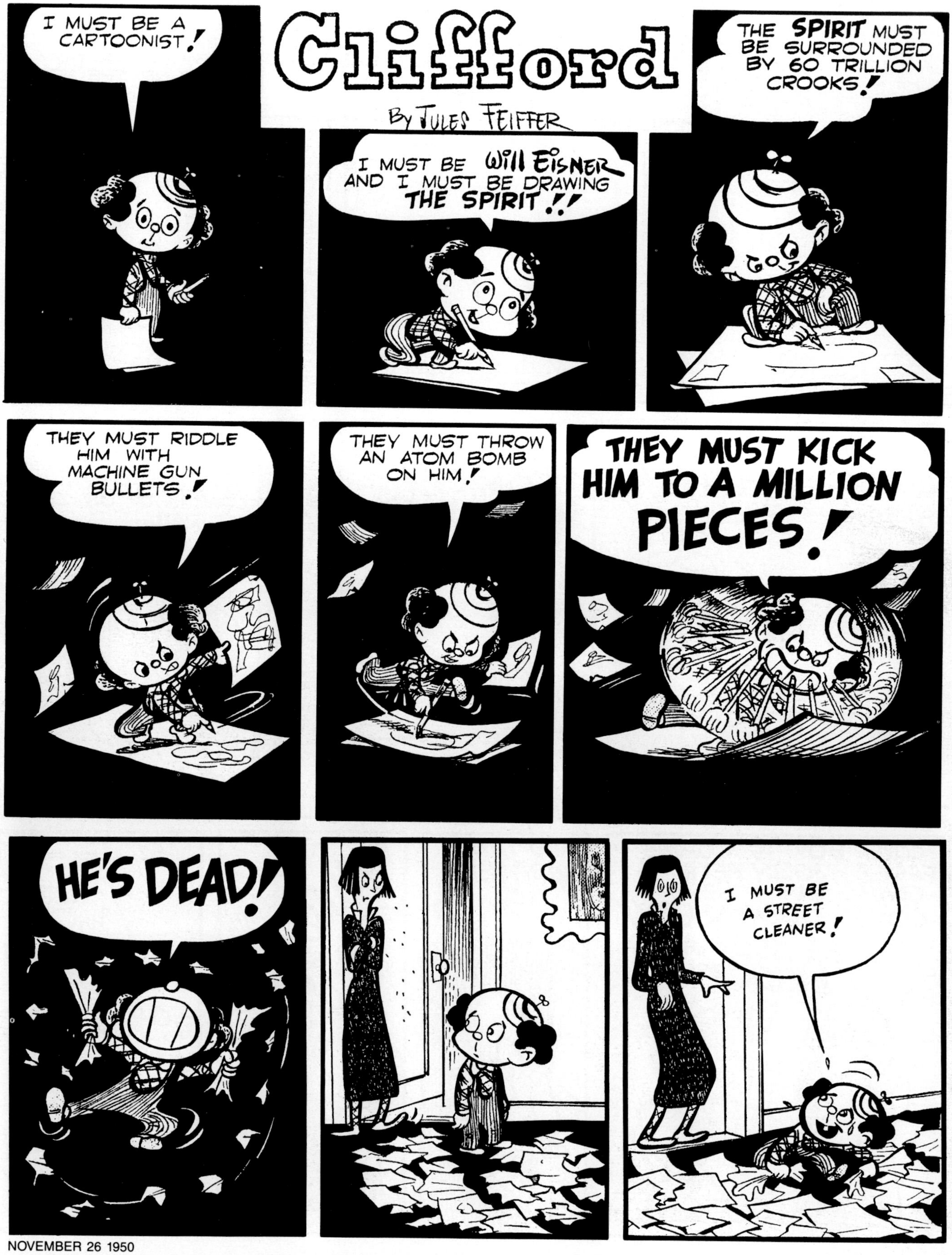
Clifford
By Jules Feiffer
I MUST BE A CARTOONIST!
I MUST BE WILL EISNER AND I MUST BE DRAWING THE SPIRIT!!
THE SPIRIT MUST BE SURROUNDED BY 60 TRILLION CROOKS!
THEY MUST RIDDLE HIM WITH MACHINE GUN BULLETS!
THEY MUST THROW AN ATOM BOMB ON HIM!
THEY MUST KICK HIM TO A MILLION PIECES!
HE'S DEAD!
I MUST BE A STREET CLEANER!

NOVEMBER 26 1950

Clifford

By Jules Feiffer

DECEMBER 3 1950

Clifford

By Jules Feiffer

DEAR SANTA CLAUS!

WELL, HA HA, SANTA OL' KID, ANOTHER YEAR HAS ROLLED AROUND AND GOOD OLD CHRISTMAS IS AROUND THE GOOD OLD CORNER!

YES SIR, SANTA I BET YOU KNOW HOW US KIDS LOOK FORWARD T'SEEING YOU EVERY YEAR AND I BET YOU JUST THINK IT'S BECAUSE YOU BRING US GIFTS!

WELL, SANTA, OLD PAL, OLD BUDDY, THAT JUST AIN'T SO! NOPE!! WHY, FOR ALL THE KIDS ON THIS BLOCK CARE, YOU DON'T HAFTA BRING US ANY GIFTS THIS YEAR!

SO DON'T GO OUT OF YOUR GOOD OLD WAY, SANTA, SAVE YOUR GOOD OLD MONEY. I DON'T KNOW HOW IT IS WITH OTHER KIDS, BUT FOR ALL THE KIDS ON THIS BLOCK CARE....

...DON'T BRING US A THING! BY THE WAY, SANTA, HOW IS THAT DEAR LITTLE OLD MRS. CLAUS! I HOPE SHE IS IN FINE HEALTH. REGARDS FROM ALL THE BOYS. Clifford

P.S., OH, I ALMOST FORGOT OUR TEACHER, MISS GUSH SAYS SHE'S GOING TO FAIL ALL OF US UNLESS WE GET BETTER MARKS SO MAYBE IF YOU COULD HAVE A LITTLE TALK WITH HER....

THINK IT'LL DO ANY GOOD?

I DUNNO... MY FATHER CALLS IT DIPLOMACY!

ALL WE C'N DO IS HOPE!

Clifford

By Jules Feiffer

DECEMBER 17 1950

Clifford

By Jules Feiffer

HO HO HO!! IF IT ISN'T "LITTLE" CLIFFORD! MERRY CHRISTMAS!

YAWN!

HO HO HO! IT'S ME, SANTA CLAUS! I'VE BROUGHT YOU A GIFT!

YAWN...STICK IT OVER IN THE CORNER, LIKE A GOOD JOE, WILL YA?

HO HO HO! HOW SANTA LOVES LITTLE BOYS! HERE YOU ARE CLIFFORD, A DOLL!

A WHAT!

A DOLL!

NOW LOOK, BUSTER, IF YOU'RE GONNA WAKE ME UP JUST TO GIVE ME A DOLL, I.... WHAT ELSE YOU GOT???

WELL, I HAVE HERE A NICE WOOLEN SWEATER, GENUINE MATERIAL, MARKED DOWN FROM...

I DON'T WANT A SWEATER!

LET'S SEE, HERE'S A MONOGRAMMED CREEPALONG HAGGERTY GUN HOLSTER, COMES IN FOUR ATTRACTIVE COLORS, ORANGE, GREEN, MAROO...

I GOT IT! WHAT ELSE...

HMMM.... HOW ABOUT A 100% COWHIDE PENCIL HOLDER, DESIGNED TO WITHSTAND ANY KIND OF WEATHER, IT....

DO YA HAVE A "SUPER-SHOT ANTI-SUBVERSIVE ATOM BLASTER"?

N--NOT ON ME!! NO...

UH HUH- AND I DON'T S'POSE YOU HAVE A "MARVEL COMBINATION JET ATOM THROWER AND MINE SWEEPER".

N--NO, I DON'T!

YAWN SORRY SANTA, MAYBE NEXT YEAR, HUH?

"SURPRISE HIM" YOU SAID! "GIVE THE KID A THRILL" YOU SAID! WHAT KIND OF A FIEND ARE WE RAISING ANYHOW?

SHHHH!

DECEMBER 24 1950